To order copies
Amazon.com
BarnesandNoble.com

From the Hood - America at Risk

Copyright: 2020 by Elie V. Parker

All rights reserved. No part of this work may be reproduced, stored in a retrieval system, transmitted in any form by any means electronic, mechanical, photocopy, recorded or otherwise without the prior permission of Elie V. Parker.

Dedication

This book is dedicated to George Floyd and the millions of others who have been killed, beaten, jailed, and denied basic human rights.

I have written many articles about poverty and injustice and have presented them in this book in chronological order based on or around a date the events occurred.

Title of Book

"From the Hood - America at Risk"
By Elie V. Parker

Contents

Chapters: **Page**

1) **Injustice** 11

- July 14, 2013 - Trayvon's death not in vain
- September 21, 2013 - 12 down. How many more to go?
- May 2, 2014 - Dear Commissioner Silver
- August 15, 2014 - Black boy shot by white cop
- December 4, 2014 - Ferguson Mo shooting never again
- July 6, 2015 - Power of the purse and the confederate flag
- October 7, 2017 - Tara Allen sang, 'Justice is coming soon
- October 17, 2017 - To Don Lemon - Those with the most wealth receives the most justice.
- October 19, 2017 - NFL - the new patriots
- October 25, 2017 - Justice is not free
- October 29, 2017 - Justice is for sale in America and you need the money to buy it
- August 11, 2018 - Charlotteville
- January 21, 2020 - Justice in America, if that's what you call it
- January 21, 2020 - Lawless
- May 10, 2020 - Killing of Ahmaud Aubrey and Justice in America
- May 26, 2020 - Kent State shooting May 4, 1970, four dead students
- May 30, 2020 - George Floyd killing - past time for blacks to act
- May 27, 2020 - Inequality in America and what to do
- May 31, 2020 - Racism from sea to shining sea
- June 2, 2020 - Save me slogans
- June 11, 2020 - The confederate statues tumbling down
- June 14, 2020 - Black lives matter - Do they?

Chapters:	Page
2) **Wealth**	**24**

- October 8, 2013 - Flip phone to wealth
- October 18, 2013 - Dear Richard D. Wolff
- February 3, 2014 - Slave master mentality
- May 1, 2014 - Build baby build
- June 16, 2014 - Opportunity in ownership
- July 13, 2015 - Poverty - the real problem
- June 27, 2016 - Wealth gap between blacks and whites
- September 9, 2016 - Colin Kaepernick and racial injustice
- February 21, 2017- Bill Cosby was right
- February 21, 2018 - The grand conspiracy - institutionalized poverty
- March 22, 2018 - Clyde W. Vaughan Jr., Central State University
- May 29, 2018 - African Americans and people of color need an agenda of their own
- February 14, 2019 - Mary Radcliffe - donations to newspapers
- March 7, 2019 - San Francisco Bayview
- July 11, 2019 - Gambling exploitation of the poor
- July 28, 2019 - Net worth black vs white
- January 29, 2020 - African American poverty rate
- February 15, 2020 - Wealth will set you free
- April 14, 2020 - Black people will get out of poverty
- May 26, 2020 - Lady in the woods
- June 1, 2020 - Marijuana - supposedly harmless drug
- October 6, 2005 - Katrina, an early coronavirus ignored

Chapters: **Page**

3) Health 44

- November 27, 2012 - Fiscal cliff and the VFW
- December 13, 2012 - Health responsibilities
- June 12, 2013 - Dear Nize Kasravi
- March 27, 2014 - Health chart
- March 28, 2014 - Affordable Care Act
- May 27, 2014 - Smoking and Ebony Magazine
- July 20, 2014 - Straighten California menu labeling law
- October 19, 2014 - Sugar industry
- July 21, 2017 - Coca-Cola
- January 9, 2019 - You are what you eat
- May 21, 2019 - Low fat diet reduce risk of breast cancer
- July 10, 2019 - Vaping
- November 27, 2019 - Marijuana
- January 20, 2020 - Health information
- January 22, 2020 - National reading label day
- January 24, 2020 - Health causes
- January 27, 2020 - Health alert
- February 4, 2020 - Read and protect your health
- March 27, 2020 - Coronavirus prevention
- May 27, 2020 - Coronavirus - A killer

4) NAACP 59

- January 24, 2013 - NAACP Focus
- April 29, 2014 - NAACP and NBA Owner Donald Sterling
- October 10, 2014 - NAACP Speech
- May 10, 2014 - NAACP's Agenda
- May 27, 2014 - Economic Opportunity best served Black
- July 21, 2014 - C. W. Brooks- President/CEO NAACP
- July 22, 2014 - Economic Opportunity best served with self-determination
- Oct 15, 2014 - George Holland, Pres- Oakland NAACP
- January 14, 2020 - NAACP Oakland branch - Health
- January 20, 2020 - NAACP Health Info dissemination
- January 22, 2020 - National Reading Label Day
- January 27, 2020 - Health Alert

Chapters:	Page
5) **Media**	**70**

- April 28, 2013 - Sports Analyst and talk show host influence on young people.
- July 29, 2013 - Don Lemon
- February 5, 2014 - Shaved Heads
- March 2, 2014 - So Proud to Be a Slave
- April 2, 2014 - Letter to the editor "Affordable Care Act"
- July 31, 2014 - Wolff and credibility
- September 11, 2014 - White on Rice
- October 12, 2014 - National Football League TV coverage
- October 7, 2016 - Black Man's hair
- July 3, 2018 - Claws, the TV show on TNT is racist
- July 28, 2019 - Shaved Heads Again
- February 24, 2019 - Black Face and Harvard University

6) **Education**	**79**

- April 8, 2020 - Broken english
- April 21, 2020 - Prisons before schools
- May 29, 2020 - Sports and education for blacks
- May 29, 2020 - Northeastern Ohio. Buckeyes everywhere.

7) **Gun Control**	**82**

- December 14, 2012 - Repeal the 2nd Amendment
- January 13, 2013 - Gun control
- January 16, 2013 - Gun-free society
- June 9, 2013 - Santa Monica killing and the gun-free society
- May 25, 2018 - Gun-free society
- December 8, 2017 - Elected leaders: one killing too many
- February 26, 2018 - Saving the lives of our children

8) **Coronavirus**	**87**

- May 5, 2020 - The party is over
- May 19, 2020 - Coronavirus vs the beach

Chapters:		Page
9)	**Hate**	88

- February 3, 2012 - Gay marriage
- July 8, 2018 - Name calling

10)	**Leadership**	89

- January 24, 2013 - President Obama
- September 6, 2013 - Syria - With leadership comes responsibility
- December 12, 2019 - Trump has violated the golden rule

11)	**International**	91

- July 28, 2014 - Fairness in Israel and Palestinian coverage
- July 30, 2014 - Don Lemon - Peace is at hand
- July 30, 2014 - Liz Kearney
- Aug 15, 2014 Israel & Palestine - The two state solution
- July 21, 2014 - The children are coming
- September 21, 2019 - Brexit
- October 8, 2019 - NBA in China
- October 15, 2019 - Hong Kong protest
- January 30, 2020 - UK exits EU a hollow victory
- May 27, 2020 World without borders

12)	**Conflict of Interest**	97

- Police and crime reduction
- Education and graduation
- Charities and poverty reduction
- Church and peace
- Campaign contribution and voting record
- Sales and profits
- Doctors and patients
- Lottery money for schools
- War and profiteering
- Sports in college
- Marijuana vs profits

Conclusion 99

- The end of the USA empire?
- Racism structurally embedded
- African Americans must build their own economic system
- US separated by race
- Hope in interracial marriages
- US is at a crossroad - racism or democracy

Acknowledgments 101

Bibliography 101

Index 102

Preface

The killing of George Floyd on May 25, 2020 seems to have spark an outrage in the nation unseen since the Rodney King beating by the California Highway patrol. Maybe the slow strangulation of George Floyd by an officer sworn to serve and protect it's citizens exposed the racial inequality that has existed below the surface of consciousness in the minds of white Americans but all too real in the lives of black Americans.

Officers of the law who declared themselves judge, jury and executioner may have been too much for white Americans who hold themselves out as a nation of justice and equality for all. There was no justice on the streets of Minneapolis, Minnesota that day and it was obvious in America and throughout the world. So how did we get here?

Injustice did not start on 25 May 2020. Racism, hate, inequality, poverty has been a part of America from the day it was created. It is a disease that has the potential to place the United States of America on the endangered species list. A list populated by other fallen empires such as the Roman, Egyptians, British and the Nazis all destroyed from outside or from within.

I have fought for justice and equality for the last 60 years starting with support for the open housing laws. To write a book that covers injustice in America over the last 60 years would result in a book too heavy to carry so I have restricted this writing to the last eight years. It is my hope that America can achieve justice and equality for all and truly be the democracy that the nation and the world needs.

My educational background is a bachelors of science in business administration in accounting and economics from Youngstown State University in Youngstown Ohio and a masters degree in business administration and finance from DePaul University in Chicago Illinois.

I served in the United States Army from 1968 to 1970, which included a year in South Vietnam. I received the National Defense Service Medal, Vietnam Service Medal w/4 Bronze Stars, Republic of Vietnam Campaign Medal and the Army Commendation Medal.

I worked for United Airlines for 31 years in various accounting, financial and auditing functions.

I am the author of the book "No Excuses - A Guide Out of Poverty" found on Amazon.com.

Elie V. Parker

Chapter 1 - Injustice

July 14, 2013 - Trayvon's Death Not in Vain

Let us build together a world free of fear and mistrust to prevent future Trayvon Martin shootings. A quality education for all would be a good first step to achieve this goal.

September 21, 2013 - 12 Down. How many more to Go?

The recent shooting of 12 people on a Chicago basketball court reflects the status of the African- American in the United States.

May 2, 2014 - Dear Commissioner Silver

Racism is the enemy of Democracy. Your actions removing Donald Sterling from the NBA is commendable but Sterling was supported and nurtured by the NBA for years even though he had a history of racism. Polices should have been in place to prevent Sterling from owning a NBA team in the first place. This problem seems to go deeper than Sterling. What should by addressed is the culture of the NBA and how it allowed racism to permeate its organization. You, the owners and the players need to determine the underlining causes of racism and put in place guidelines to prevent this from happening again.

August 15, 2014 - Black boy shot by White Cop

We have been to this rodeo before. Cop shoots Black boy, community riots, politicians promises change, there is no change or it is ineffective, national press leaves town until next Black boy is shot by a cop.The reason that the shooting does not stop is because the changes are usually superficial and do not address the real problems of the community.

Chapter 1 - Injustice

The circle of violence is just repealed over and over which is why we have the Oscar Grant killing in Oakland, or the Trayvon Martin killing in Sanford, Florida or the countless other killing in the Black and poor communities.

You probably noticed that most of the killings occur in the poor neighbors and in order to stop the killing you have to eliminate the root cause of the shooting. The root cause is poverty. The way you end poverty is to ensure that each person receives a quality education.

December 4, 2014 - Ferguson, MO Shooting Never Again

Recently, I was invited to participate in a march to protest the shooting of Michael Brown, a Black teenager in Ferguson, MO by a police officer. Previously, I was also invited to do the same for other shootings like Trayvon Martin in Sanford, FL and Oscar Grant in Oakland, CA. Although we have taken to the streets shooting after shooting, these marches don't seem to be doing much good since the shootings have not stopped. I think we need a different strategy. Instead of marching in the streets, we should march to the schools and libraries and learn English, math and science and earn a high school diploma and a college degree. Then start businesses, create jobs and end poverty. Since most of the people being shot are poor, once we end poverty we will probably be able to declare Ferguson, MO Shooting Never Again.

July 6, 2015 - Power of the Purse and the Confederate Flag

The power of the purse can bring about justice and equality to South Carolina. There is nothing more powerful in this greed filled world than the dollar bill, or its sisters, the pound sterling, Euro, Yang or the peso. Just as boycotts brought an end to apartheid in South Africa, boycotting the companies that operate in South Carolina will bring about an end to the Confederate flag and the bigotry that it stand for.

Chapter 1 - Injustice

Determine which companies operate under the Confederate battle flag in South Carolina. When you purchase their products you support hate, racism and slavery. When you boycott their products you strike a blow for freedom.

October 7, 2017 - On the video Tara Allen sang 'justice is coming soon'.

Blacks have been singing this song for at least 300 years and yet justice has not arrived. It is time to realize in United States, justice is not free it must be paid for. You pay for justice just like you pay for anything else, you buy it. Black people need the money to buy justice and in order to have money, African-Americans must go into business and create jobs and wealth.

You can sing and pray all you want but the only thing that matters in America is wealth. With wealth you buy justice.

October 17, 2017 - To Don Lemon - Those with the most wealth receives the most justice.

It feels good to say we are a just nation. It feels bad to say we are an unjust nation. So we go about the world saying that we are a just and equal nation and at the same time fill up our prisons with young black men. Young Black men without the resources to post bond or hire good attorneys to keep them out of jail. They must rely on a poorly paid public defender. Whose budgets are for ever being cut.

At the same time, a person of wealth can post bond, hire the best attorneys and if convicted can even receive a lighter sentence or on appeal have the case thrown out altogether. After all, this same wealthy person contributed to the judge's campaign.

Justice is not free but it can be bought. Blacks need the resources to buy justice.

Chapter 1 - Injustice

October 19, 2017 NFL - The New Patriots

In 1776, the founding fathers of the United States gathered to form a more perfect union. They risk scorn and fortune to protest injustice and unfair treatment by the king of England. Today, Colin Kaepernick and other NFL players are not so unlike the original protesters of this nation. They also risk scorn and fortune to protest injustice. Just as we celebrate our original founding fathers protest, we should celebrate and support the NFL players efforts to form a more perfect union. The players know that without justice we are all at risk.

A nation without justice is like a ship without a rudder, aimlessly wandering the vast seas of irrelevancy until it crashes upon the rocks and sinks into extinction.

October 25, 2017 - Justice is not Free

Call in Kaepernick and his band of patriots seeking justice in America.
Martin Luther King and millions of others have fought and died for equal rights and yet in 2017 justice for all has not been achieved. Kneeling, singing, praying and marching has failed to bring justice to all Americans. Marauding police forces and white vigilantes beat, strangle and kill young black American males with impunity. Someone once said that freedom is not free. I have come to the conclusion that justice is not free but it can be bought.

October 29, 2017 - Justice is for sell in America and you need the money to buy it.

You buy the best attorneys, you buy the favorable juries, you buy the judge, you buy the Congress people who write the laws and you buy the police who enforce the law. It is one big supermarket and you need the cash to own it all. Blacks need to accumulate money to buy and build the businesses that produce the goods and services that generates profits.

Chapter 1 - Injustice

Money controls America. Those who have it controls those who don't.

The more money you have the more justice you get.

The first settlers came to America because they were tired of paying most of their money to the kings and queens of Europe.

Slaves were brought to America because the plantation owners didn't want to pay the high cost of labor associated with picking cotton.

America is business and business is America. Those who own the businesses of America own and control America.

August 11, 2018 - Charlottesville

You don't have to go to Charlottesville to witness hatred, intolerance and racism because it is all around us. It is usually cloaked in coded apparatus and carried out in our companies, churches and government. It is police profiling, Hollywood stereotyping, poor schools and high incarceration rates for people of color, jobs, housing and banking discrimination. Every possible opportunity to put people of color down has been employed. From slavery to Charlottesville, the nation has not progressed very far. Bigotry is as much a part of America in year 2018 as it is in 1860. It is ingrained in adults, children and soon as possible the newborn. It is the one thing the United States has been unable to overcome in over a century and possibly the thing that will eventually destroy it. The United States like other empires may be destroyed from within. Whites, Blacks Asians, Hispanics only marrying, hiring and living within their own race. Each building walls around each other transforming the United States from a possible democracy to a segregated and weaken collection of small countries.

Chapter 1 - Injustice

January 21, 2020 - Justice in America, if that's what you call it.

The judicial system is demonstrably corrupt and undemocratic. A system bought and paid for by the highest bidder. Despite overwhelming evidence of criminal activity by Donald Trump, the system chose to do nothing.

January 21, 2020 - Lawless

When lawless rains democracy drowns. No one is above the law except the king of the United States, Donald Trump. The Republican Senate by not allowing witnesses and evidence in the impeachment trial has anointed Donald Trump king of the United States.

May 10, 2020 - Killing of Ahmaud Aubrey and Justice in America

Justice in America is not given it must be purchased just like any other valuable commodity. When Blacks buy the judicial system which includes the judges, jury and the police, they can then control the outcome. Those with the most money get the most justice.

May 26, 2020

Kent state shooting May 4, 1970, 4 dead students

I was stationed in Fort Hood Texas having just returned from a one-year tour in South Vietnam. The army offered at three months early out if you attend college. I decided to take them up on it so on May 3, 1970, I visited the campus of Kent State university in Ohio In pursuit of a Master's degree.

Chapter 1 - Injustice

There was a Vietnam war protest on the campuses at that time and the Ohio national guard was present on the campus grounds. Although the national guardsmen were armed, there appeared to be a friendly coexisting between the soldiers and the students. The students were even putting flowers into the barrels of the National Guard rifles. All seemed calm and I thought that maybe I will attend this school. Of course the next day all hell broke loose and four students were killed by the national guard.

I decided that it might be safer in the army than in college and put in the extra three months of my enlisted time. The Master's program would have to wait.

May 30, 2020 - George Floyd Killing - Past Time for Blacks to Act

As long as we continue to blame white people for our problems, the problems will remain.
We continue to expect white people to change but we are unwilling to change and they are a convenient scapegoat to blame for the lack of our actions.
The killing of blacks, the high black unemployment rate and the high black poverty rate will continue until black people take control of their community. To take control of our communities we must build our businesses, schools and vote into office local, state and federal governments that will justly and fairly represent us.

May 27, 2020 - Inequality in America and what to do about it.

The Civil Rights Act of **1964** was enacted July 2, **1964**. The act outlaws discrimination based on race, color, religion, sex, or national origin. Ending discrimination in hiring should have ended poverty in the black community but in more than a half of a century later the poverty rate for Blacks is almost 3 times the national average. Also Black unemployment is nearly twice the national average. What happened? In two words, very little.

Chapter 1 - Injustice

The tactics used to create the civil rights act, marches, boycotts and civil disobedience ended official job discrimination but not actual job discrimination. The stereotypes and beliefs of those in power did not change. For example when I was in high school, I asked my bookkeeping teacher if there were any jobs in industry that required a bookkeeper. I was told no. What my teacher was really saying is that there were no white-collar jobs for Black people in industry.

Because of the riots, the marchers, Martin Luther King and the other civil rights leaders, I landed a white collar job in a fortune 500 company. Prior to the civil rights act this company had not hired one black financial management person in its 40 year history. I was a trailblazer and did not realize it. In fact an Hawaiian who had been hired earlier advised me that the White employees had refused to sit next to him.

This was the degree of job discrimination in America in 1970. When I first started with the company I was given no job training. I think I had been forced on my manager and he had no desire to see me succeed and therefore offered no training. As the work piled up on my desk and I have no idea what to do with it, I started to flounder until a white woman in the department stop by my desk and asked if she could help. She saved my you know what, as did other White managers.

Unfortunately, for the next 31 years it was a running battle with other White managers who were trying to get me fired. The fate of other Black employees were worse than mine. Most of the African Americans that were hired after me were demoted, fired or just driven out of the company.

The civil rights laws were still on the books but the commitment to enforce them quickly disappeared under an avalanche of Republican Party efforts to decimate the affirmative action programs. These programs represented the action side of the civil rights law.

Chapter 1 - Injustice

So here we are today, civil rights laws ignored, Black and other people of color with poverty and unemployment rates higher than the national average, Black men chased down the streets by cops and vigilantes and murdered without fear of punishment, black leadership using 1964 set-in tactics to fight 2020 economic battles, and a national education system that produces more Blacks, Hispanics and American Indian service employees than scientists and engineers.

My solution:

1. Instead of Blacks and other people of color seeking jobs at White companies they should build their own companies.
2. Justice is not free it must be purchased. The judges, police and even the jury must be purchased just like any other valuable commodity.
3. Black leadership and Black people must become more economically oriented. Emphasis need to be placed on more bankers, accountants, entrepreneurs, business people, financiers, insurance brokers and all of the other business careers that are required to run an economic system.
4. Education is key. You must control the education system if you want the system to work for you. This will require voting to put in office mayors, governors and presidents that are in tune to your community needs and your educational requirements.

The civil rights act is only as effective as a people who believe in it and in the United States that is a small minority. People of color must take control and ownership of their communities if they are to achieve civil and economic rights.

May 31, 2020 - Racism From Sea to Shining Sea

March 3, 1991 Rodney King beaten by the California Highway patrol, cops who were acquitted.

Chapter 1 - Injustice

February 4, 1999 Amadou Diallo was shot 19 times by New York City cops who were acquitted. May 25, 2020 George Floyd killed by Minnesota cops, soon to be acquitted if history is any guide. From The Statue of Liberty to Santa Monica pier to the Everglades to the Land of the Lakes, Black people are beaten, shot and strangled with impunity by White cops. White juries do not convict White people for killing Black people. Justice in America goes only as far as the color of your skin.

America is a racist country even though it likes to call itself a democracy. You don't have to look too far to see this. Of the fortune 500 companies, only four are headed by Blacks. There are no Black governors in the United States. There are two Democratic Black US Senators. The top military leaders are all White. There are no Black representatives on the US Supreme Court. There is one on the Supreme Court who looks black but he votes more against Blacks than the White members of the supreme court. The major media's are own and control by Whites. The major sports teams are almost all owned by Whites, although many of the players are Black. Most of the college coaches are White, although many of the players are Black.

Ownership and leadership positions are almost exclusively White which is how they control the media, the financial markets, the Congress, the White House, and the judicial system down to the jury selection which acquits the cops who beat, shot and suffocate Black people.

Solution for Black people or any one else who is oppressed is obvious. The solution is ownership. If you don't own your community then someone outside of your community will own you. Equality will come when you build the businesses to deliver it.
So let's get started.

Over $1 trillion pass through Black hands every year, more than enough to fuel every conceivable type of commerce that can be developed or purchased. We only have to capture these dollars and recycle them back through the Black community just as White communities do. We can capture this market by establishing a motto of honesty, integrity and quality goods and services.

Chapter 1 - Injustice

Once we gain control of our communities, we will have the resources to purchase justice including the politicians, judges and juries.

Justice in America sounds good but it's justice in word only.

June 2, 2020 - Save Me Slogans

Black Lives Matter, Do not Shoot, I'm Black and I'm Proud, I am Somebody. These slogans seem to be the catalyst that black people believe will propel them from poverty into prosperity. They seem to believe that playing on a person's sympathy will gain them access to justice and equality. This thinking is further from the truth.

Soliciting sympathy is not seen as an avenue to success but a recognition of failure. Begging is seen as a weakness not a strength and over the course of human events it is strength that has brought change not weakness. Blacks have for too long believed that there was good and justice in the human being and that by appealing to the goodwill of the oppressor their burden of poverty would be lifted from their shoulders. With this type of thinking in place, Blacks do not seem to think that there's anything for them to do but wait for deliverance. Well in the last 300 years, deliverance has not shown up and there's no indication that it will ever show up until blacks create their own deliverance.

In these modern times that means blacks must create their own economy. A economy that includes businesses, schools and governments. In other words they must do the same thing the Europeans and Asians did.

These groups do not wait for the deliverance but went out and created the deliverance. In their native countries they were some of the poorest people on the planet but they came to America and built businesses and structures to propel them into becoming some of the richest people in the world.

Chapter 1 - Injustice

To prosper in America, you must produce. Subjugating yourself to beggars is the opposite of production. In order to get out of poverty, Blacks and any other poor groups must build companies, corporations, law firms, businesses, large farm associations and all of the other industries that produce income and wealth.

In America with income and wealth you can buy justice and equality by donating to a governor, mayor or judges election. These are the officers that selects the chief of police or hire the police officers. If police officers know that they work for you , they would be less inclined to suffocate, shoot or kill Black people or anyone else for that matter.

The slogan that I would recommend is Build baby Build.

June 11,2020 - The Confederate statues come tumbling down.

Down come the Confederate statues. Racism is no more or at least one is lead to believe. The problem is that racism is not in statues. Racism is in the people who put the statues up and those folks have not gone anywhere.

Symbols of change is not change. Often you get these symbols of change after riots or protest. After the Watts protest, the United States formed the Warren commission. The Commission made recommendations to combat racism. The effectiveness of these recommendations is reflected in the size of the protest in 2020. In other words, in 30 years little has been done.

If America was truly interested in ending racism it would start a quota system. A quota system would require companies to maintain a job force on each job level that reflects all of the people of the country. The advantages of a quota system is that it is measurable and you can award or punish those who made the quota.

Absent a quota system, the country will probably continue to migrate to a tribal system based on race.

Chapter 1 - Injustice

June 14, 2020 - Black Lives Matter - Do They?

Black Lives Matter, Black Lives Matter, Black Lives Matter. We have been chanting Black Lives Matter for years. During that time, Blacks continue to be killed by white cops or white vigilantes. Chanting Black Lives Matter do not make it so. The reality is Black Lives do not matter. If Black Lives mattered, we wouldn't have to keep chanting it year in and year out. Racism is what matters in the United States. It permeates almost all institutions. From the boardroom to the courtroom, from birth to death, from altar to pew, from sea to shining sea.

Chapter 2 - Wealth

October 8, 2013 - Flip Phone to Wealth

I was watching the NFL Monday Night football game the other day and they showed the billionaire Jerry Jones, the owner of the Dallas Cowboys football team, using a cheap flip phone and not an expensive smart phone. It dawned on me that those of us who have not made our first billion dollars and own smart phones could traded down to the less expensive phone and save thousands. A prepaid flip phone cost about $8 a month. A smart phone cost over $90 a month depending on options. The difference is $82 a month or $984 per year. The average price of a home in the United States is $200,000. There are available government home loans that require only a 3% down payment or $6,000 dollars. Using a flip phone and not the smart phone a person can save enough money in about six years to make a down payment on a home. Home ownership is one of the best ways to build wealth and family stability. It has been said that poor people can not escape poverty due to a lack of funds. Maybe the flip phone is one way out.

October 18, 2013 - Dear Richard D. Wolff

On 10/18/2013, I listened to your presentation on Capitalism and Inequality on KPFA 94.1 radio in the San Francisco area.

I agree with your point on how the system works but I also think that capitalism can play an important role in ending inequality and poverty. Also I believe that those in need, need to do the most to get out of poverty. After all, they are the ones who stand to gain the most by escaping poverty.

I have written a book called "No Excuses - A Guide Out of Poverty". The book recommends the use of a business strategy to end poverty. The poor will be required to get a college degree and start their own businesses which will create jobs and build wealth. I know it is not easy to earn a degree but I did it and without funds from my parents, scholarships or loans. I did have to work part time for eight years to earn a BSBA and MBA.

Chapter 2 Wealth

My book also stresses the need for the poor to not engage in activities that harm their chances for success like using drugs, drinking, smoking, breaking the law or following an unhealthy eating life style. In your presentation, you mention that Blacks have a high rate of obesity which often comes from eating foods with a large amount of salt, fat, cholesterol, sugar and calories. No one is forcing Blacks to eat this unhealthy type of food. It is up to them to realize that following an unhealthy diet can contribute to obesity, illness and costly medical bills that can keep a person poor and out of a job.

My book can be purchased on Amazon.com for a small amount.

Keep your opinions coming on KPFA 94.1, they are what a true Democracy requires.

February 3, 2014 - Slave Master Mentality

African Americans need to shake the slave master mentality.

Under slavery, the slave master provided housing, food and a job to Blacks. Today that dependency has not changed much. Blacks still expect others to provide for their housing, their food and their job. As long as Blacks do not provide for themselves they will always be slaves.

To break out of the dependency on others, Black people will have to build their own housing, grow and harvest their own food and build companies that hire Blacks.

To accomplish these goals the first step is to learn a skill by earning a college degree, or acquire knowledge through on-the-job training or using other methods that will give you the tools needed to start a business or advance in your current job.

The next step is to pool your education and financial resources and build companies that are trustworthy, have integrity and deliver quality products and services.

Chapter 2 Wealth

When you are the master of your own destiny, you will not be a slave to any one.

May 1, 2014 - Build Baby Build

Keeping the faith is not going to end racism or poverty. Even after decades of trying to end bigotry, the previous owner of Los Angeles Clippers, Sterling's racist beliefs are still alive and well in America. I think we should stop trying to change others and start changing ourselves.

Instead of responding to the agenda of bigotries which as you can see is a waste of time and resources, we should execute our own agenda. Our agenda should include building our own businesses, companies, corporations, industries and even sport teams. When we are the owners, the ranting and raving of a mad man will be drowned out by the success of our business acumen.

June 16, 2014 - Opportunity In Ownership

How many times will African Americans ask corporate America for jobs? For decades we have begged for employment in their companies and for years they have responded the same way, hell no. By now we should have gotten the message that we are not wanted in their companies. Our opportunities are not with these companies but with our own companies.

The Black Enterprise magazine May 2014 issue stated that African Americans have over 1 trillion dollars in purchasing power. With that kind of power, we do not have to ask anyone for anything. We already have the dollars to build African American companies large enough to hire every Black person in the country. Let's seize the opportunity and start an investment fund with the purpose of creating our own corporations and build our way out of poverty.

Chapter 2 Wealth

July 13, 2015 - Poverty - The Real Problem

The poverty rate for African-Americans is 27%, the highest in the nation. It has been the highest for years and yet you hear little about it. Instead the news is full of protest about the police shooting Black kids, confederate flags, and 'I Am Somebody' campaigns. These are diversions from the real problems and solutions. You can end all of the police shootings, lower every confederate flag and have a constitutional amendment declaring that every Black is somebody and still African-Americans will have the highest poverty rate in the nation. We need to ignore the diversions and get down to the problem which is poverty. By ending poverty you will end police killings. After all, how often do you hear of a rich kid being shot by the police.

Ending poverty is not that difficult. First you speak standard English which will enable you to learn how to read and write. Second you apply that knowledge to earn a college degree. Preferred degrees would be in banking, accounting, finance, economics, marketing, business law, computers, science, engineering and math. Third you use that degree to start a business. Fourth you grow the business and create wealth.

This is not a new idea. Poor immigrants have been coming to this country for centuries and doing what I described above and now they are the millionaires and billionaires of the country.

African-Americans have the most incentive to end poverty since they/we have the most to gain. Poor Hispanics who have a poverty rate of 24% and poor Whites with a poverty rate of 10% can also use the above approach.

Build Baby Build

June 27, 2016 - Wealth Gap Between Blacks and Whites

Blacks in the United States continue to lag far behind whites in key areas of economic well-being like wealth, income and homeownership, per a new report from the Pew Research Center.

Chapter 2 Wealth

While these trends have been consistent for decades, what's particularly notable is that these disparities between blacks and whites persist regardless of the level of education they attain, said Juliana Horowitz, an associate director of research at Pew.

"Even when we only look at people with bachelor's degrees, we still see these gaps," Horowitz said.

Take income. In 2014, the median household income for whites was $71,300 compared to $43,300 for blacks. But for college-educated whites, the median household income was $106,600, significantly higher than the $82,300 for households headed by college-educated blacks, the report found.

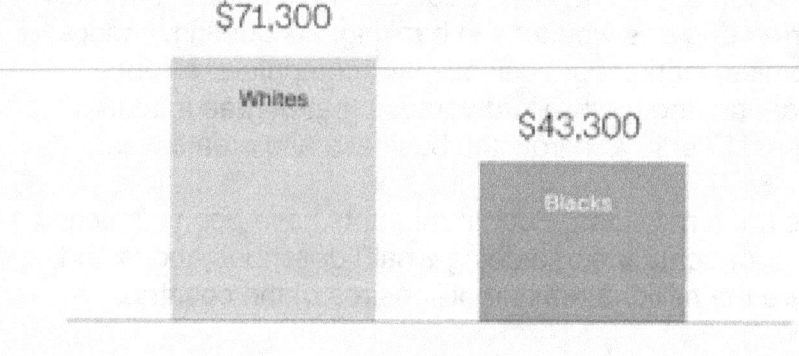

These differences are magnified when looking at overall wealth, which takes into account the value of assets like homes, retirement savings and income minus any debt owed against those assets.

The report found that in 2013, white households in the U.S. had a median wealth of $144,200 --almost 13 times the median wealth of black households at $11,200. But here again is an example where the gap is not significantly narrowed by education.

Chapter 2 Wealth

White households headed by someone with a college degree have a median wealth of $301,300 compared to college-educated black households, which have a median wealth of $26,300.
Related: Black wealth not protected by homeownership
One of the biggest ways to amass wealth, especially for people of color, is to own a home. Yet the homeownership rates for blacks is just 43% compared to 72% for whites.

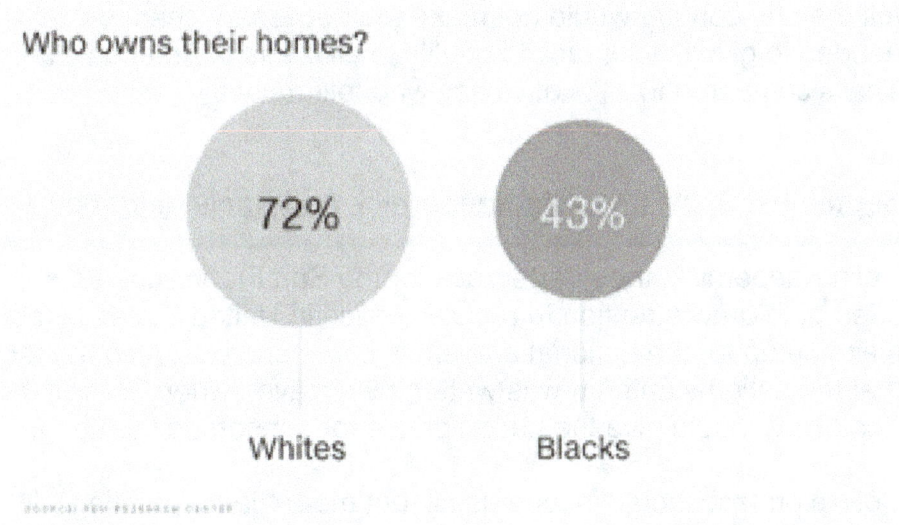

Who owns their homes?

72% Whites

43% Blacks

Homes owned by blacks also tend to appreciate less in value than those owned by whites, particularly if they are in black communities that experienced high rates of foreclosure. Historically, neighborhood segregation and "redlining" -- the practice of not investing in or providing financial or other services for communities with high percentages of black residents -- have exacerbated this trend. Blacks were also targeted with subprime loans during the housing boom and, as a result, lost a tremendous amount of wealth after the market crashed.

Even though the poverty gap between blacks and whites has narrowed, Pew found that Blacks were still at least twice as likely as whites to live in poverty or be unemployed. And while 23% of blacks said they sought food from a food bank or pantry in the past 12 months, just 8% of whites said they did so.

Chapter 2 Wealth

More than two-thirds of blacks surveyed (70%) said racial discrimination was a major reason why some blacks have a hard time getting ahead in the U.S. More specifically, 60% said they felt like they were treated unfairly compared to whites when applying for a loan or a mortgage and 53% said they were treated unfairly at work.

Perhaps the most telling statistic was that 43% of blacks said they felt that the country would not make the necessary changes needed to give blacks racial equality in all areas of American life. That's compared to 11% of whites who felt that way.

September 9, 2016 - Colin Kaepernick and Racial Injustice

Colin Kaepernick, the quarterback for the San Francisco 49ers, attempt to draw attention to racial injustice in United States by not standing up for the national anthem is commendable. Also the fact that the national anthem was written by a slave owner, Francis Scott Key should give the nation pause for supporting the song.

Colin's protest should inspire us all, but more than protesting will be required to end racism. After all African-Americans and others have been marching and boycotting for decades and yet today the unemployment rate for African-Americans is nearly twice that of white Americans. The poverty rate for African-Americans is almost 3 times the rate for white Americans. The net worth of white America is 10 times more than the net worth of black America.

African-Americans can overcome these disadvantages by doing what other disenfranchised groups have done and that is to accumulate wealth. Wealth controls America. With wealth you can select the police chief or the corporate president or through business ownership determine who is hired or promoted. You can build wealth by owning assets, businesses, corporations and industries.

By creating wealth through business ownership we can overcome racial injustice. Make an investment in yourself and build baby build.

Chapter 2 Wealth

February 21, 2017 - Bill Cosby was right

As African-Americans slip further and further into economic and social chaos, it has become abundantly clear that the current methods of fighting poverty has failed. The nearly 4000 shootings in Chicago in 2016 of which 674 were fatal, the unemployment rate for African-Americans at nearly twice the national average and the poverty rate of 27% for African-Americans is ample proof that a change in direction to fighting poverty is needed.

For too long African-Americans have depended on the government and the established business community to provide us with jobs, education and sustenances. Because of this dependency, we have the worst schools, the lowest paying jobs and unsafe neighborhoods. The solution to the problem is clear, we must start to depend on ourselves and take responsibility for our actions. That's where Bill Cosby comes in. Now I know there's going to be some blowback because I said that Bill Cosby was right. After all, he has been vilified in the press but I believe in this case and probably in most cases the message is more important than the messenger.

No matter what you think of Bill, his words in 2014 are as true today as they were then when he spoke of the need for African-Americans to take responsibility for our actions and that is why I have repeated them below.

In addition to Bill Cosby's recommendations, I want to add my own which includes the need for African-Americans to build a $1 trillion investment fund to be used to build African American businesses that will create jobs and generate prosperity in the black community.

It Is time for African-Americans to take action and save our communities.

Elie Parker

Chapter 2 Wealth

BILL Cosby HAS GONE AND DONE IT AGAIN...

'They're standing on the corner and they can't speak English.
I can't even talk the way these people talk:
Why you ain't, ...
Where you is,
What he drive,
Where he stay,
Where he work,
Who you be...
And I blamed the kid until I heard the mother talk.
And then I heard the father talk.
Everybody knows it's important to speak English except these knuckleheads. You can't be a doctor with that kind of crap coming out of your mouth.
In fact you will never get any kind of job making a decent living.
People marched and were hit in the face with rocks to get an education, and now we've got these knuckleheads walking around.
The lower economic people are not holding up their end in this deal.
These people are not parenting. They are buying things for kids. $500 sneakers for what?
And they won't spend $200 for Hooked on Phonics.
I am talking about these people who cry when their son is standing there in an orange suit.
Where were you when he was 2?
Where were you when he was 12?
Where were you when he was 18 and how come you didn't know that he had a pistol?
And where is the father? Or who is his father?
People putting their clothes on backward:
Isn't that a sign of something gone wrong?
People with their hats on backward, pants down around the crack, isn't that a sign of something?
Isn't it a sign of something when she has her dress all the way up and got all type of needles [piercing] going through her body?
What part of Africa did this come from??
We are not Africans. Those people are not Africans; they don't know a thing about Africa .....

Chapter 2 Wealth

I say this all of the time. It would be like white people saying they are European-American. That is totally stupid.

I was born here, and so were my parents and grand parents and, very likely my great grandparents. I don't have any connection to Africa, no more than white Americans have to Germany, Scotland, England, Ireland, or the Netherlands. The same applies to 99 percent of all the black Americans as regards to Africa. So stop, already! ! !

With names like Shaniqua, Taliqua and Mohammed and all of that crap .... And all of them are in jail.

Brown or black versus the Board of Education is no longer the white person's problem.

We have got to take the neighborhood back.

People used to be ashamed. Today a woman has eight children with eight different 'husbands' -- or men or whatever you call them now.

We have millionaire football players who cannot read. We have million-dollar basketball players who can't write two paragraphs.

We, as black folks have to do a better job.

Someone working at Walmart with seven kids, you are hurting us. We have to start holding each other to a higher standard..
We cannot blame the white people any longer.'

~Dr.. William Henry 'Bill' Cosby, Jr., Ed..D.

February 21, 2018 - The Grand Conspiracy-Institutionalized Poverty

Some institutions benefit from poverty. They might even fight against the elimination of poverty.

Chapter 2 Wealth

Listed below are some of the institutions that should be investigated to ensure that they are not promoting and profiting from the poor.

1) Liquor Industry
2) Churches
3) Police
4) Courts
5) Lawyers
6) Prisons
7) Republican Party
8) Democrat Party
9) NRA
10) Military
11) Businesses
12) Charities
13) Welfare Offices
14) Civil Rights Organization

March 22, 2018 -

Clyde W. Vaughan Jr.
Acquisitions Specialist
Hallie Q. Brown Memorial Library Central State University

Dear Clyde W. Vaughan Jr.,

Thank you for adding my book "No Excuses - A Guide Out of Poverty" to your collection. I believe that by applying the recommendations in this book, we can end poverty.

Also the more the recommendations are used the sooner poverty will end.

I would like to gift my book to other universities, civil rights groups and any other organizations fighting poverty.

Could you provide me with a list of such organizations?

Chapter 2 Wealth

May 29, 2018 - African Americans and People of Color Need an Agenda of their Own

African Americans have the highest poverty, unemployment and incarceration rate in the country. This has been the situation for decades and much of this could be because Black Civil Right Organizations spend a great amount of time and resources reacting to someone else's racial agenda. For example when Blacks were arrested at Starbucks in Philadelphia, Black Civil Rights Organizations spend time and money denouncing the restaurant. Also when the Wells Fargo Bank was charged with discrimination, Blacks denounced the bank, again. This is not the first time the bank has been denounced for discrimination because Wells Fargo has been sued over and over again in the past for its racial lending practices. The law suits have not changed the racial policies of the bank. Also going to the other large banks will not end racial discrimination because their lending policies are similar to Wells Fargo.

Citigroup, JPMorgan and Bank of America have all been sued for discrimination in lending practices and there is nothing to indicate that these lending institutions will stop discriminating against people of color. What Blacks and other people of color need is their own agenda. An agenda that builds and owns banks, restaurants and all the other commercial enterprises that build wealth and stability. Ownership of business by African Americans and other people of color will ensure an end to racial discrimination and poverty.

Educate-Build-Repeat

February 14, 2019 - Mary Radcliffe- Donations to newspapers

I am reluctant to donate to your newspaper.
Donations will only make you dependent on the next donation.
On the other hand, investments will generate income for your next investment. I am willing to invest in your newspaper. Of course, I want a financial return on my investment (ROI).

Chapter 2 Wealth

Also I want the Black community to move away from non-profit enterprises and into profit making businesses. Profits propel small companies into large corporations that can then hire thousands of workers from the community. Also the larger your corporation, the more influence you have on your environment, your politicians, and your future.

You may also want to merge and incorporate with other like-minded media companies.

Once you have incorporated, let me know so that I can invest in you.

March 7, 2019 - San Francisco Bay View

Mary Radcliffe

Economic Racism

The San Francisco Bay View headlines are disturbing. They are replete with injustice and police shootings. The problem is I could probably go back over the last 50 years and find the same headlines. It is as if we have not advanced in half a century. It could be that we have not advanced because we are using the same tactics over the last 50 years and are getting the same poor results.

Other groups have come to America and faced racism but they have overcome it. Take for instance the Bank of America which was founded as the Bank of Italy by Amadeo Pietro Giannini in 1904 in San Francisco to provide banking services to Italian immigrants who faced banking discrimination.

African-Americans will also have to build their own banks, Insurance, retail companies, etc., like the Italians, the Germans, and Asians did if they ever expect to end economic racism and poverty.

Chapter 2 Wealth

July 11, 2019 - Gambling exploitation of the Poor

I recently was at a birthday party in Cleveland Ohio. The party was held at a racetrack where casino gambling was permitted. As I left the party, I could not help but observe the people on the gambling floor. The tuxedo wearing gamblers as presented in the movies were nowhere to be found here. Hunched over the machines in tattered apparel were poor people hoping for a miracle win but with the odds stacked against them. Cities and states have justified legalized gambling on the premise that taxes from the establishments would help the poor. From what I could see, gambling was not helping the poor but exploiting them. Cost benefit analysis should be required before any gambling is legalize to ensure that the benefits from gambling Is greater than its cost.

July 28, 2019 - Net worth Black vs White

To cover these high college tabs, students are taking on more debt. Black students have less family wealth to draw on according to one analysis, the median wealth of white families in 2016 was $171,000, compared with $17,409 for black families and so they often need to borrow more.

In 1983, the median wealth of white families overall was $105,369, compared with $13,324 for black families. By 2016, the divide had widened to $171,000 for white families and $17,409 for black families.
Today, the average white family has $157,884 saved for retirement, while the average black family has just $25,212.

January 29, 2020 - African-American Poverty Rate

African American Poverty Rate: 21.2% (9.0 million people)
Percentage of African Americans who fell below the poverty line in 2017

Hispanic Poverty Rate: 18.3% (10.8 million people)
Percentage of Hispanics who fell below the poverty line in 2017

Chapter 2 Wealth

White Poverty Rate: 8.7% (17.0 million people)
Percentage of non-Hispanic Whites who fell below the poverty line in 2017

Native American Poverty Rate: 25.4% (700,000 people)
Percentage of Native Americans who fell below the poverty line in 2017

Per talk poverty.org

February 15, 2020 - Wealth will set you free.

In 1863, the Union army broke through the confederacy lines at Gettysburg and marched south to free the slaves. A century and a half later the promise of that day has not yet fully arrived. Blacks once bounded by chains are now bound by poverty. Black poverty rates are over 20%, twice the national average. The Black unemployment rate of 6% is nearly twice the national average.

Through most of the last 50 years, marches, protests and laws against discrimination in employment, housing and public accommodations have done little to lift millions of blacks out of poverty.

The reason why blacks are still in poverty is because we have not build a business economy. America is business and business is America. If you're not in business in America you'll probably find yourself in poverty which is where we find millions of black people.

We cannot march our way out of poverty but we can build our way out.

We need to change Black History Month into Black Business Month.

Wealth will set you free. Until we own, we will forever be slaves.

Chapter 2 Wealth

April 14, 2020 - Black people will get out of poverty.

Black people will get out of poverty when they stop expecting White people to do what Black people need to do for themselves such as speaking standard English which Is the foundation for learning (science and math books are written in standard English), earning a college degree and building businesses that create jobs and wealth. Also Blacks need to stop doing things that reduces wealth such as alcohol, drugs or tobacco consumption. Blacks spend over 60 billion per year on these items. Blacks also should stop consuming unhealthy food. Unhealthy food has high amounts of sodium, fat, cholesterol, calories and sugar and can lead to obesity, heart attacks, strokes and diabetes and increased health costs and death. The CDC has stated that these underlying health conditions has contributed to a higher coronavirus death rate among Black people.

May 26, 2020 - Lady in the woods

I joined my father's drill team that was sponsored by the Elks club in Youngstown, Ohio. The practice drills took place on the other side of town so I had to cross an open field in order to reach the practice area. As I maneuver my way through the woods and brush, I heard a faint voice crying for help. It came from a very thin woman laying on the ground. I asked her if she needed help and she said that she had been driven from her home and forced into the woods. I offered to take her back to her neighborhood and because she was so weak I had to carry her. I asked her where did she live and she pointed to one of the places I never wanted to enter. In Youngstown that place was called the monkeys nest. It was one of the most nastiest and dangerous places to live in the town. I did have a great amount of trepidation going into this area but my concern for her overcame my concerns for myself.

As I carried her up the broken glass and bottle filled street, where poorly clothed and malnourished kids played in the dirty streets, I asked her where does she live. She pointed to a building that was not a house but was actually a saloon. I took her inside and placed her on her feet.

Chapter 2 Wealth

A very large man came up to us and with one swing of his large hand slammed the woman to the floor. Once he had flatten her, he turned toward me in a fit of rage as if I was causing him problems for bringing her home. Me at age 15 and about 100 pounds less than the body slammer, I decided it was time for me to depart monkeys nest.

As I raced out the door of the salon, pass the broken glass and dirty streets and the malnourished and poorly clothed children, I made a pact with myself that one day I will return and clean up the streets, clothe the children and most importantly ensure a woman's right to life, liberty, and the pursuit of happiness.

To that end I have supported the women's right movement in all aspects of life including the right to higher education, The Me too Movement, abortion rights, right to top management positions and most importantly the right to live without fear.

June 1, 2020 - Marijuana, supposedly harmless drug.

In 1968, my fellow soldiers and I were headed back to our bunker in South Vietnam. Suddenly, we came under mortar attack. We all took off for the bunker. As we approached the bunker one of our fellow GIs was standing on top of a bunker with his arms raised up to the sky welcoming in the incoming mortar and rocket rounds. He was stoned out of his mind with marijuana. We grabbed him and pulled him inside the bunker as the rounds started to land. The marijuana had made him unaware of the dangers that were raining down on top of him. When I hear that marijuana is not a dangerous drug I always think back on that day in South Vietnam when drugs did almost cost a life. To say the drugs are dangerous or mind altering is only part of the story. The other part of the story is how they can affect you financially, mentally, and your quality of life. After all many companies require a drug test before they hire you. If you can't pass a drug test you're not likely to get the job or the financial gains and medical benefits the job might provide. The cost of drugs is another great impediment to your financial well-being. Over 193 billion is spent on illicit drugs per the NIH. Bottom line, do not let drugs dictate your health or your financial future.

Chapter 2 Wealth

October 6, 2005 - Katrina an early coronavirus warning ignored.

African Americans die in disproportionate numbers due to the coronavirus. Many reasons have been given including the lack of healthcare, the history of health problems and the lack of adequate health facilities in the African-American community. This may all be true but the question is why is it true. How did it come to this where African-American communities are so exposed to the coronavirus?

This is not the first calamity to inflict damage on the African-American community. Back in 2005 there was another storm in the community called Katrina that roared into New Orleans and in particular the ninth ward where many African-American lived and killed hundreds. In the more affluent communities of New Orleans, residence with means were able to flee the stricken city and save their lives. Many of the black residents of the city who did not have the resources to leave either drowned or packed into a stadium unfit for human life. After the tragedy, I wrote the following article:

"Katrina Exposes Poverty and Opportunity 10/6/2005

Katrina reveals poverty in Black America. Of course Blacks know it was there all along. Forty years after the war on poverty it is clear that in the Black community, poverty won. Over the same period, White America has gone on to build their wealth, businesses and communities, while nearly twenty five percent of the Black population has remained under the poverty line. Black unemployment is twice the rate of Whites and in almost every category Blacks have not done well. Blacks have the lowest reading and writing scores and highest incarceration rate. They eat the worst food often high in sodium, fat, cholesterol and calories and have the highest obesity rate. They have the lowest home ownership rate and least assets. Even though over 500 billion dollars pass through Black hands every year, Blacks do not own one fortune 500 company.

Chapter 2 Wealth

One other thing Katrina revealed, if you are Black and poor do not expect an unfriendly or incompetent government to come to your aid. America is a nation of power. If you have the power you can save yourself, if you do not, you drown. Blacks need power and in America, business is power. Business creates jobs, wealth and gives you the resources to send your child to college or to flee a hurricane. In New Orleans, poor Blacks did not even have a car to escape the storm.

For decades, Blacks have depended on Whites to provide them with education, housing and jobs. The high poverty and unemployment rate in the Black community has shown that this approach has failed. Blacks should stop waiting for White America to provide for them. Blacks need to provide for themselves and they can by building the infrastructures required to sustain and grow their communities.

Black organizations like the NAACP, Rainbow/ Push Coalition, CORE and SCLC should convert from the civil rights wars, which they have won to creating Black businesses and wealth. Blacks need to build banks to control the money supply, communication companies to control the media, corporate farms to control the food supply.

Blacks need to build and own every type of business that impacts the Black community. From these businesses, Blacks can create jobs, build schools, create wealth and finally end poverty. It can be done, White America has done it and they are rich and prosperous. Black America must do it so that they too can be rich and prosperous.

When another Katrina comes along and she will, if Blacks have taken their destiny into their own hands and have built the resources to get out of harm's way, they will be able to weather any storm whether it comes in the form of an economy slow down, a racist or inept government or just a really bad butt- kicking hurricane like Katrina."

Fast forward to today.

Chapter 2 Wealth

The African-American community ignored the opportunity to prevent another Katrina catastrophe. The NAACP, Rainbow/Push Coalition, CORE, SCLC and the other black organizations continued to fight a civil rights war and ignored the economic war. They did not build their businesses, schools, health facilities but continue to rely on white America to provide these services. The results are tragic. The coronavirus has swept through the black communities killing blacks in a disproportionate number to their share of the general population.

Since Katrina, blacks did not prepare for the next Katrina which came in the form of the coronavirus. The only question now is will African-Americans learn from the coronavirus pandemic and build their own economy or will they once again depend on the white man to save them.

Chapter 3 - Health

November 27, 2012 - Fiscal Cliff & The Veterans of Foreign Wars (VFW)

Recently I visited a VFW bar. The bar was filled with veterans doing what people do at a bar, consuming drinks. Now you might wonder what does this have to do with the fiscal cliff? For one thing, the veterans who probably are receiving government medical benefits were consuming a product that is harmful to your health. If the drinking causes a medical problem, which in many cases it does, the VA, Medicare or some other government agency may be required to cover the cost of treatment. By the government supporting the VFW's bars, they are also increasing the cost of medical coverage and adding to the fiscal cliff.

There are many examples where government action or lack of action has added to the fiscal cliff. Listed below are some steps the nation can take to reduce medical cost and at the same time increase the health of the nation.

1) Smoking cost the nation 450,000 lives and $53 billion dollars a year. We should ban smoking in all public places & tax tobacco companies and smokers an amount equal to the cost of smoking.

2) The cost of government medical coverage should be based on the amount of coverage a person uses. The more medical services you use the greater your cost. This will encourage people to live a healthier life style.

3) Companies and governments should not have to pay medical expenses caused by an unhealthy life style.

4) Any company or organization that sells or distributes food or drink should be required to list the amount of cholesterol, salt, calories, fat and sugar in the product. This will encourage the food industry to develop a healthier food supply. Also with greater knowledge of what is in the food supply, the public can make healthier food choices.

Chapter 3 Health

Through good health management we can turn the fiscal cliff into the highway of personal and financial health.

December 13, 2012 - Health Responsibilities

Should a person be held responsible for their actions? If a person creates a health problem like liver disease, lung cancer, or diabetes by drinking, smoking, or becoming over weight or obese should the government or a company pay to treat a preventable disease. Or should the person who created the problem in the first place be held responsible? Also, if there is no penalty for unhealthy choices, what incentive is there for the person to change. Does the government or a company pay over and over until the whole health system is bankrupted and there are no longer resources to treat even the health problems that are not preventable?

There should be a price to pay for unhealthy activity. The health system including Medicare and Medicaid and businesses should move from a standard payment amount for all to an incentive payment plan where the person who lives the healthy life style pays less than the person living the unhealthy life style. After all, an unhealthy life style means higher health risk. The greater the risk the greater the cost to the medical system. Also the greater the cost to the individual, the more incentive that person has to live a healthier life which reduces the cost for preventable diseases and increases the resources available to treat diseases that are not preventable.

June 12, 2013 - Dear Niaz Kasravi

The best and surest way to get something done is to do it yourself. If we need housing, we should build housing. If we need jobs, we should create companies. If we need good health, we should eat healthy. It is all up to us and it should be.

Chapter 3 Health

March 27, 2014 - Health Chart

Free yourself from the diet that leads to poor health, illness, and death.

Currently over 50,000 people die each day due to an unhealthy eating habits. One hundred thousand Americans fall ill due to eating food with excessive amounts of fat, cholesterol, sugar, calories, sodium. Although the government requires large food producers and restaurants to list the food ingredients in their products, restaurants with locations under 19 and smaller food producers are not required to list food ingredients.

To live a healthier and a longer life, people should have full knowledge of what is in the food and drink they consume. It should not matter if you are eating at a national chain restaurant or your local restaurant, for your own health you have a right to know what is in the food you are eating. When you are aware of what is in the food being offered, you can make healthier food choices. Healthier food leads to a healthier person which reduces health cost. Someone once said an ounce of prevention is worth a pound of cure. With health care cost running in the billions of dollars and threatening to destroy Medicare, and balloon private medical cost, there could be no truer saying. Prevention can reduce the cost of medical coverage and save lives and Medicare.

We need a law to strengthen the current Federal law to include food labeling for all food sellers.

March 28, 2014 - Affordable Care Act (ACA)

I am amazed that some have worked so hard to deprive people of health care. The ACA is an opportunity for some of the poorest in our nation to improve the health of their family. The act covers emergency services, hospitalization, pre-existing conditions, prescription drugs and a host of other health care issues. A complete list can be found on the ACA web site (HealthCare.gov). As a person who grew up without any health coverage, I am very happy to support the ACA effort to bring health care to the most vulnerable in our society.

Chapter 3 Health

May 27, 2014 - Smoking & Ebony

I recently received a copy of the Ebony February 2014 issue. I appreciate your efforts to provide information and news to the African American community, but I object to your magazine advertising tobacco products. Smoking kills over 400,000 Americans each year. African Americans make up 45,000 of that total. Please stop advertising this dangerous product.

July 20, 2014 - Strengthen the California Menu Labeling Law

California's menu labeling law, California Health and Safety Code Section 114094, outlines menu labeling requirements for food facilities. The law defines a food facility as a facility that operates under common ownership or control with at least 19 other food locations.

In the state of California, millions of people are eating food that is detrimental to their health. As a result, they are getting sick or die from the ingredients in the food their bodies can not safely process, such as sodium, fat, cholesterol, sugar and calories.

The California menu labeling law requires that these unsafe ingredients be listed in food facilities. As stated above, it covers only food facilities with at least 19 locations. That leaves thousands of food outlets and millions of consumers without the protection of the menu labeling law.

Also, unhealthy food consumption drives up medical cost for the individual, the employer and the state and federal government medical plans, Medicare and Medicaid. Consumers have a right to know what is in the food they eat so they can make healthier food choices.

By eating healthier, people will live healthier lives, live longer and reduce the nations health bill. The California Menu Labeling Law needs to be strengthen to include any food outlet that serves the public.

Chapter 3 Health

October 19, 2014 - Sugar Industry

There are ballot initiatives this election that would tax sugary beverages. Not surprising the sugar industry is fighting the initiatives. Profits appear more important to them than a healthy consumer. The television ad that I saw featured three people, a White female, a Black female, and a Black male.

The male Black actor, adorned in earrings and gold chains looked more like a drug dealer than a sugar advocate. I guess the sugar industry thinks that Blacks are out breaking the law, when they are not gulping down their sugar filled products. In the ad, the Black actor is saying that the tax is against the poor since they consume much of the sugary products. Another stereotype presented is if you want to show poor people put a Black person in your ad.

July 21, 2017 - Coca-Cola

Two prominent black pastors in the Washington D.C area filed a lawsuit July 13 against Coca-Cola and the American Beverage Association, claiming soft drink companies deceive customers about the health risks of consuming their products.

"It's become really clear to me that we're losing more people to the sweets than to the streets," Pastor Delman Coates told The Washington Post. "There's a great deal of misinformation in our communities, and I think that's largely a function of these deceptive marketing campaigns."

Coates elaborated in an interview with CBS News. "The background of this lawsuit is that there's an epidemic of diabetes, cardiovascular disease and a range of other degenerative diseases in the black and Latino communities, and really throughout America," he explained. "For me, as a pastor, I see the toll it takes on families and children when they lose their parents much too soon. It breaks my heart and I'm saddened by the way in which we're losing so many people."

Chapter 3 Health

Pastor William Lamar added: "It is a matter of life and death in our communities. Marketing for Coca-Cola is focused around health and fun and showing very sexy bodies in their advertising. You never see an obese person. If the people are consuming Coca-Cola at this rate, there is no way those bodies would look like that. It's almost as if they are selling joy. They are equating this product with the things that people are hoping for -- joy, smiles, family. But this product will not deliver that. It delivers the exact opposite. Silence around this issue is violence."

January 9, 2019 - You are what you eat.

Obesity rates in the United States has reached epic proportion's. Illness and deaths attributable to overweight conditions include strokes, heart attack's, and diabetes. The main reason for the overweight reconditions is the amount and type of food we eat. The way to reduce the chances of death and illness due to the food we eat is to change our diet and count our calories. Counting calories is not difficult. Federal law requires that most foods purchased identify the amount of calories in each product. Also to maintain a healthy diet the amount of sodium, cholesterol, fat and sugar is included in the labeling.
A healthy diet, along with a daily exercise routine will go along way toward a longer and healthier life.

May 21, 2019 - Low fat diet reduce risk of breast cancer

I am concerned about the health of the population.
Recently I ran across an article titled "Low fat diet that helps reduce risk of dying from breast cancer by Erika Edwards. I believe that the more people know about what's in the food they eat, the better and healthier food choices they can make. Most foods in our grocery stores are labeled with their content. Large chain restaurants also must provide a list of the contents in the food they serve. The smaller restaurants do not have to provide such information. That's where I believe we have a weak link in our health information system. I would like to see bills passed on the state and federal level requiring that all food outlets provide the contents of their products. The information should include the amount of sodium, fat, cholesterol, calories and sugar.

Chapter 3 Health

Information should also include the daily recommended amount of each ingredient. Not only will a healthier diet eliminate or reduce breast cancer but it will also reduce heart attacks, strokes, diabetes and cancer of the liver, colon, pancreas, lung and many other types of cancer. The more information the consumer has about his or her health, the healthier the person, the community and the nation will be.

Also the healthier we are the less we have to spend on health costs which runs into the billions of dollars each year for individuals, companies, and governments. In some companies, the health bill alone for their employees is unsustainable. Often the employees' benefits are cut or the deductibles are increased. Individuals who become ill or involved in accidents and are without health insurance puts a financial strain on themselves, their families, and government assistant programs.

I am personally committed to ending breast cancer since my sister died from the disease. A disease that with better dietary information we can eliminate.

We can have a healthier future, we only have to believe in it.

July 19, 2019 - Vaping

The city of San Francisco has just banned the sale of vaping products. I applaud this action. Recently there was an article opposing the ban because of its perceived negative effects on the African American community. Not vaping can only improve the Black community and any other community for that matter.

Today the African-American community has the highest unemployment and poverty rate in the nation. We do not need another vice to add to this problem. What we do need is for African-Americans to commit time and effort to speak standard English which facilitates textbook learning, earn a college degree, land a good job or start a business. Doped up with vaping will not allow us to achieve these goals.

Chapter 3 Health

Also, African-Americans and other parts of the population spend billions of dollars on products that are detrimental to their wallet and their health such as alcohol which causes pancreatic cancer or tobacco products that causes all kinds of cancer such as lung, mouth, esophagus, throat and liver. Addictions to marijuana, cocaine, and gambling also reduces net worth. Food and drinks with high levels of cholesterol, fat, calories, sodium and sugar causes strokes, heart attacks, obesity and diabetes. This type of consumption reduces our net worth. We need to spend our money on income producing assets such as a college degree, buying a house, starting a business and investments in stocks and bonds.

Spread the word our financial future and our health is in our hands.

November 27, 2019 - Marijuana
If you want to keep control of your body stay clear of those substances that control you like alcohol, tobacco, cocaine, opioids, and marijuana.

January 20, 2020 - Health information
The more people know about what's in the food they eat the healthier choices they can make. By reading the food and drink ingredient labels, we can identify products that have a high unhealthy level of calories, fat, cholesterol, sodium, and sugar. These are the main ingredients that contribute to heart attacks, strokes, obesity ,and diabetes. Any food or drink above the recommended healthy daily amount should be discouraged.

We can inform the community of what is healthy or unhealthy through social media including Facebook, Twitter and YouTube as well as newspapers, newsletters, Television ads, and Radio. By providing better health information, we can make a major contribution to the health of our community and the country.

January 22, 2020 - National Reading Label Day
The health of the United States is in crisis. A large percentage of our population is overweight and obese. Heart attacks, strokes, and diabetes is a curse on all of our communities.

Chapter 3 Health

The cost of treatment including drugs and hospitalization is on the rise with no end in sight. I believe that one way to address this massive problem is to adopt a prevention protocol. A program that will inform the population of what is in the food they are eating and drinking to enable them to make more healthier choices.

I am calling for a National Reading Label Day. National read the label day is a day when we read the ingredient label on the food and drink we are purchasing or we have already purchased. The calories, fat, cholesterol, sodium, and sugar in each serving is then compared with the NIH and CDC recommended consumption per day and adjustments to your daily consumption can be made accordingly.

The national recommendation daily consumption for men is as follows:
Calories - 2500
Total fat - 80g
Sat. Fat. - 25g
Cholesterol-300mg
Sodium 2300-mg
Sugar added-37.5g
For African-American men 1500 mg of sodium is advised.

The recommendation daily consumption for women is as follows:
Calories - 2000
Total fat - 65g
Sat. Fat. - 20g
Cholesterol-300mg
Sodium 2300-mg
Sugar added-25g

These are recommendations for the average individual and you should consult with your doctor or even check the Internet to see what's best for you.

National Reading Label Day is created to inform the public of the nutrition information available to them so that they can make better health choices. The more health information we have, the more healthier choices we can make.

Chapter 3 Health

Three steps to a healthier life:
Read the label.
Know what is in the food and drink you consume.
Follow the NIH and CDC health guidelines.

January 24, 2020 - Health Causes:
At a Glance from the national institutes of health (NIH)

- A study found that biological risk factors—including weight and fat around the abdomen—are primarily responsible for higher rates of diabetes for black Americans compared with white Americans.
- The study suggests that making positive changes in known risk factors, like losing excess weight, can help reduce the racial health disparity for developing diabetes.

January 27, 2020 - Health Alert
"National Reading Label Day" campaign
Obesity, diabetes, and high blood pressure that leads to heart and kidney disease is at crisis levels, see chart below. The chart shows that 47% of the black population is obese. Other races are not that far behind. Obesity, Diabetes, and High Blood Pressure:

Race	Obesity	Diabetes	High Blood Pressure
Black	47%.	20%.	42%
Hispanic.	46%.	21%	29%
White.	38%.	13%.	28%
Asian.	12%.	14%.	27%

Source: Center for disease control (CDC)
These negative outcomes can be reversed if we read the nutrition labels on the food and drink we consume and follow the daily recommended amounts of calories, fat, cholesterol, sodium, and sugar. Excess amounts of these ingredients are major contributors to diabetes, obesity, high blood pressure, heart attacks, strokes, and kidney disease.

Healthy people live longer, have fewer illnesses and pay $1,400 less for health costs. Knowing what's in the food you eat is an easy and cheap way to improve your life.

Chapter 3 Health

Read your way to a healthier and richer lifestyle and join the "National Reading Label Day" campaign.

February 4, 2020 - Read and Protect Your Health

Let it be said of all of us, we knew what had to be done and we had the strength and courage to do it.

Read the label and save your health and your money.

Protect your health and your wealth. Read the label.

March 27, 2020 - Coronavirus-Prevention

The coronavirus pandemic will affect all of us. Our families, our jobs, our health, our daily activities will all feel the pandemic. Worldwide, as of March 26, 2020 there are 526,000 coronavirus cases and 23,700 deaths from the virus. The United States has 82,400 cases and 1,100 deaths and counting. No one really knows when the virus will be stopped. The Centers for Disease Control and Prevention (CDC) has made recommendations on how to protect yourself from the virus which includes avoiding social gathering, work or study from home, avoid discretionary travel and practice good hygiene such as washing your hands, avoid touching your face, sneeze or cough into a tissue or the inside of your elbow and disinfect used items and surfaces frequently. All of these recommendations will hopefully slow down the infection rate with proper hand washing being one of the critical actions recommended. See below information from CNN Health on the effective way to wash your hands. To read the complete article go to the CNN Health website "Why soap, sanitizers and warm water work against Covid-19 and other viruses."

The saying that we are all in this together has never been more relevant. The life you save may not only be your life but the lives of your family members, friends and neighbors.

Stay Safe

Chapter 3 Health

CNN article - What soap and warm water do.

Under the microscope, coronaviruses appear to be covered with pointy spires, giving them the appearance of having a crown or "corona" -- hence the name. Beneath the crown is the outer layer of the virus, which is made up of lipids, or what you and I would call fat.

Now imagine that coronavirus is your butter dish, covered with buttery fat. "You try to wash your butter dish with water alone, but that butter is not coming off the dish," Dr. William Schaffner explained. "You need some soap to dissolve grease. So soap or alcohol are very, very effective against dissolving that greasy liquid coating of the virus.

What does getting rid of that outer layer do to the germ?
It physically inactivates the virus, so it can't bind to and enter human cells."

May 7, 2020 - Coronavirus - A killer

The coronavirus is a killer. It does not care about what race you are, your religion, your income, or any of the other contrived delineators concocted by man. The coronavirus is a equal opportunity killer and at this time it has killed over 260,000 people worldwide and 75,000 people in the United States. Also, as of today there is no treatment or vaccine. The only thing that seems to work is testing, tracking and social distancing. Or in other words, if you can't beat it, hide from it in your home.

This approach may keep you safe but there are financial consequences that might make you poor. One solution is for the federal and state governments to make sure that no one starves or is made homeless and to develop a vaccine which would allow the country to safely reopen and rebuild.

Chapter 3 Health

The African-American community ignored the opportunity to prevent another Katrina catastrophe. The NAACP, Rainbow/Push Coalition, CORE, SCLC and the other black organizations continued to fight a civil rights war and ignored the economic war. They did not build their businesses, schools, health facilities but continue to rely on white America to provide these services. The results are tragic. The coronavirus has swept through the black communities killing blacks in a disproportionate number to their share of the general population.

Since Katrina, blacks did not prepare for the next Katrina which came in the form of the coronavirus. The only question now is will African-Americans learn from the coronavirus pandemic and build their own economy or will they once again depend on the white man to save them.

June 4, 2020 - Reparation

To: Larry Ivory - National Black Chamber Commerce Chairman

To: Robert L. Johnson - Founder and Chairman of The RLJ

I listened to your comments concerning the wealth gap between white and black America on Bloomberg news May 3, 2020. You made some valid points but what was missing is the responsibilities of black America to close the wealth gap.
We have a wealth gap because blacks have been depending on white America to provide us with jobs, education, and housing for over 300 years. Based on the wealth gap between black and white America today, it's obvious that approach has not worked.

White men did not build their companies for black people. White men built their companies to provide jobs for themselves and their sons and now their daughters. If they gave these jobs away to blacks, then their sons and daughters would be jobless and that has not happened, will not happen, and should not happen.

Chapter 3 Health

Over $1 trillion pass through black hands every year. We only have to build businesses that can capture these dollars and turn them over in the black community several times. The distinguishing characteristics of these businesses should be that they are honest, they have integrity and they deliver quality goods and services.

Our motto should not be what we expect from others but what we should expect from ourselves.

Black America's Responsibility to Close the Wealth Gap

With protesting, rioting and looting occurring in the country, America has once again turned to possible solutions to end racism. I don't have much faith in these forthcoming solutions because most of them have been proposed before like, affirmative action, more access to credit, police reform, diversity and more feelings for the poor and downtrodden.

This outpouring of sympathy for black people normally happens after each riot. Sympathy abounded after the Watt's riot of August 11, 1965, and the Rodney King riots May 4, 1992, as well as the current George Floyd killing May 25, 2020. Sympathy is appreciated, but in the past as soon as the fires burn out, the sympathy and the recommended reforms burn out with them.

Since 1965, the on again, off again so-called renewed commitment for justice and equality has only resulted in an increase in the wealth gap between blacks and whites. Currently the wealth of white America averages $171,000 per family. This compares with black America at $17,000 per family.

One of the recommendations proposed to close this gap is reparation. The problem with reparation is that it is a continuation of blacks depending on whites for their substance and it is a psychological impediment to black pride. It's hard to hold your head up with your hand out.

Chapter 3 Health

Also since whites own most of the businesses, any money the blacks receive will go right back into white hands and the black communities will be just as poor as ever. Reparation is not the solution but black entrepreneurship is.

Of the many recommendations to close the wealth gap, one that has not been mentioned is the responsibility of black America to close the wealth gap. The reason we have a wealth gap is because blacks have depended on white America to provide jobs, education, and housing for over 300 years. This dependence on white America to provide for black America is based on a false premise that white America would share with black America and other people of color the fruits of the nation.

This assumption is far from reality. White men did not build their companies for black people. You only have to look at the number of black CEOs in the top 500 companies After 50 years of affirmative action, there are only four black CEOs.

Instead of asking white America for more money in the form of reparations or more job opportunities, blacks should create jobs by building their own businesses. Over $1 trillion pass through black hands every year. Blacks need to build businesses that can capture these dollars and turn them over and over in the black community. As dollars are reinvested in the black community, jobs and income is created which would end the wealth gap, poverty, rioting and looting. The distinguishing characteristics of these businesses should be that they are honest, have integrity and deliver quality goods and services.

Black expectations should not be what they expect from others but what they should expect from themselves.

Build Baby Build

Chapter 4 - NAACP

January 24, 2013 - NAACP Focus

Thank you for the opportunity to respond to your question of where the NAACP should focus its efforts. I hope that you will continue to encourage feedback.

With Obama as President, I think that the NAACP and the African-American community have a great opportunity to end poverty. I believe we should seize this moment by depending more on ourselves. We should create jobs by building companies. We should improve our health care by eating healthy and exercising. We can increase our chances of finishing high school and college and increasing our education level by speaking standard English and learning how to read and write well. If we accomplish these things, our crime rate will decline and guns and the death penalty will be a thing of the past.

I have written a book on how we can reach these goals called "No Excuses- A Guide Out of Poverty" found on Amazon.com. I hope that the NAACP will recommend the book to the membership and the community.

If there is anything I can do to help the NAACP achieve its goals, please let me know.

We are our greatest asset, let's put it to work.

April 29, 2014 - NAACP and NBA Owner Donald Sterling

The racist views of Donald Sterling the owner of the Los Angeles Clippers NBA team have been well known for years. Nevertheless, the Los Angeles branch of the NAACP was about to honor Sterling with an humanitarian award. It has been reported that Sterling recently made a donation to the NAACP Los Angeles branch. How desperate is the NAACP for funds that they would honor the very person who insults them?

Chapter 4 NAACP

The NAACP needs to seek other revenue sources or they will forever be forced to accept the handouts of others, who disrespect them for taking or needing the handouts.

I suggest that the NAACP start their own companies and produce their own funds. Through ownership you create jobs, wealth, control and respect. Also you do not have to depend on your detractors for your survival.

October 10, 2014 - NAACP Speech

The poverty rate for African Americans is three times the rate for White Americans (27 to 9 percent).

The unemployment rate for African Americans is twice the rate for White Americans (10.5 vs 5.3 %) and have been so for at least the last thirty years.

White America has ten times more assets than Black America. Much of it in the value of their homes.

Ladies and gentlemen, boys the girls, we Africans Americans have an economy problem that is bad and only getting worse. Five years ago, the asset ratio between White America and Black America was five times and now it has double.

What is a race to do? We can march in protest in the streets. We can hope that someone or some thing will come along and save us. We can pray for welfare support. We can sing songs and hope that somehow are troubles will go away.

Actually we have done all these things and our neighborhoods have only gotten worse. The dropout rates in our schools have only increased and our prison population has only grown.

If is time for us to stop expecting others to save us. It is time that we take responsibility for our own future.

Chapter 4 NAACP

As a member of the Oakland NAACP board, I will make proposals that will end poverty and crime in the communities.

I call my program "The HEW" Health, Education, and Wealth.

1) Health:

African-Americans have one of the shortest life spans in America. Much of this is due to poor eating habits. Unhealthy eating habits causes heart attacks, diabetes, high blood pressure, cancer, and other fatal diseases. I will propose programs to enhance the health of the community.

2) Education:

Having a quality education is the foundation for success. I will work with the students, parents, and educators to ensure that every child receives the very best education.

3) Wealth:

We can build wealth by saving more than we spend, purchasing income producing assets (property, stocks, bonds), maintaining good credit, owning vs renting, and many other wealth producing actions. I well make proposals that will move us from the poorest in the nation to the richest.

I am a member of the Oakland NAACP and have previously served on its Executive board. I am also a lifetime member of the National NAACP. I would like to be considered to again serve on the Oakland NAACP board.

Elie Parker

May 10, 2014 - NAACP's Agenda

We are always responding to other people's agenda. We spend so much time addressing their racist agenda, we have little time to accomplish our own agenda. We need to take responsibility for ending our poverty.

Chapter 4 NAACP

When we are denied loans by banks, we should start our own banks.

When we are denied insurance, we should start our own insurance companies.

When we are insulted by racist NBA owners, we should start our own NBA.

May 27, 2014 - Economic Opportunity is best served Black

Dear: Hilary O. Shelton
Senior VP of Advocacy, Director of the Washington Bureau
NAACP

Someone once said that if you want to get something done you should do it yourself.

African Americans have depended on others to provide us with jobs, housing, education, security and a plethora of other needs and wants. As a result, we have the highest unemployment rate, the worst graduation rate, the poorest housing, the least secure neighborhoods, and the lowest asset base than any group of people in the United States.

The old method of depending on others to provide for us has failed. We need to provide for ourselves.

We can accomplish this by pooling our resources (currently at over 500 billion) and building our way out of poverty.

I have outlined how this can be done in my book "No Excuses - A Guide Out Of Poverty" found on Amazon.com.

Let us stop asking for help and start providing help.

Elie V. Parker

Chapter 4 NAACP

From: Hilary O. Shelton
Senior VP of Advocacy, Director of the Washington Bureau
NAACP

Elie, did you watch the President this evening?

Inequality and lack of economic opportunity are our nation's fastest growing threats, and President Obama made clear what's at stake in his State of the Union address.

Countless individuals are living in a cycle of underemployment, unemployment, and poverty they can't escape, and an inordinate number come from African American communities.

Everyone—from the federal government, to those in the private sector, to organizers like you and me—has a stake in this issue. Fixing it is the only way to guarantee a thriving, vibrant America for all.

We want lawmakers to know the NAACP community is calling for a solution to economic inequality. The message won't be complete without your signature. You can sign with just one click.

Elie, I'm not going to sit here and tell you this will be easy. There's a lot of work to do.

We are encouraged by President Obama's executive order raising the minimum wage for federal contract workers to $10.10, and we urge Congress to raise the minimum wage for all. But that cannot be all we do. We must create real living wage jobs with opportunities for advancement and job security—the types of jobs that form the foundation for our middle class.

We need to strengthen and protect the Consumer Financial Protection Bureau, as it helps preserve and expand economic viability of consumers of color and all Americans. This will remove economic barriers and throw the doors of opportunity wide open.

It won't be easy, but the fights that matter rarely are.

Chapter 4 NAACP

The President laid out an ambitious strategy tonight. Add your name to those who support this important work today:

http://action.naacp.org/economic-inequality

We look forward to working with President Obama, Congress, and with all who support picking people up, not cutting them down.

Thank you,

Hilary O. Shelton
Senior VP of Advocacy, Director of the Washington Bureau
NAACP

July 21, 2014 - Dear: Cornell William Brooks President and CEO - NAACP

Congratulation on your election. Thank you for the e-mail on your July 21, 2014 speech to the NAACP in Las Vegas.

There is no question that the NAACP was relevant in the past. The question now is how to make the organization relevant in the future.

Times have changed since the boycotts and marches. Blacks can now go to most hotels, eat in most restaurants, and live in the better neighborhoods. The big question now is can they afford to. Black unemployment is twice the national average in good times or bad. Black poverty rates are in the twenties. Even if jobs were offered to African Americans, the schools Blacks attend would not qualify them for employment.

Up to this point, the model to follow for Blacks to get out of poverty was to depend on White America to provide the education, jobs, housing, finances, and basically all the needs of the Black community.

Chapter 4 NAACP

This model has failed most African Americans. We need to take control of our communities. We need to build and control the schools. We need to build the companies that create the jobs. We need to build the banks that finance our businesses.

Is the NAACP relevant? It will be if we make it so. I have written a book "No Excuses - A Guide Out of Poverty". It can be found on Amazon.com. I have also included a copy with this letter.

My book outlines how we can be relevant. So relevant that the question will not come up again.

Thank you

Elie V. Parker
Life Time NAACP member

July 22, 2014 - Economic Opportunity is best served with Self-Determination

Dear: Roslyn M. Brock
Chairman, NAACP National Board of Directors

Someone once said that if you want to get something done, you should do it yourself.

African Americans have depended on others to provide us with jobs, housing, education, security, and a plethora of other needs and wants. As a result, we have the highest unemployment rate, the worst graduation rate, the poorest housing, the least secure neighborhoods, and the lowest asset base than any group of people in the United States.

The old method of depending on others to provide for us has failed. We need to provide for ourselves.

We can accomplish this by pooling our resources (currently at a trillion dollars) and build our way out of poverty.

Chapter 4 NAACP

I have outlined how this can be done in my book "No Excuses - A Guide Out Of Poverty" found on Amazon.com

Let us stop asking for help and start providing help.

October 15, 2014 - George Holland - President of the Oakland Branch of the NAACP

Thank you for taking my call and listening to some of my concerns about the African-American community. You stated at the NAACP general meeting on 10/11/14 that although the nation has elected its first Black President Barack Obama, we still have many problems to overcome. Among those problems is the fact that the African-American poverty rate at 27 percent which is three times the rate for White America. Also the Black unemployment rate of 11 percent is twice as high as it is for the White population.

I am committed to ending poverty and I believe that you and the NAACP share that commitment. The obstacles to overcome are many but the need to are boundless. I believe that the best way to end our poverty is for us to take charge of our future. We need to control our schools, businesses, and jobs. Also we need to stop doing the things that harm us like using illegal drugs, drunkenness, and consuming unhealthy food. This effort should be shared by all, but those who have the most to gain, need to do the most.

January 14, 2020 - NAACP Oakland Branch

Thank you for addressing the health crisis in our community. There is one area that you may not have addressed in your NAACP Oakland Health Committee Questionnaire survey and that is greater access to health information. Knowing what's in the food you eat and acting on that information can greatly improve the health of the community. Currently, food purchased in the grocery store has to identify the amount of sodium, cholesterol, fat, sugar, and cholesterol in the product. This is also true for the chain restaurants, but not restaurants with a small number of locations.

Chapter 4 NAACP

I think we should make the community more aware of the labeling information on food and encourage them to purchase only the healthiest food. Also we can make the community aware of the national recommendations on the amount of cholesterol, fat, sodium, and sugar in your daily diet. We can kick the campaign off with a national read the label campaign.

In addition, we could work to have the federal and state governments require that all food and drink be labeled as far as the amount of sodium, cholesterol, calories, fat, and sugar in the product.
I look forward to working the NAACP to achieve these goals and as one great man once said:

"You must be the change you wish to see in the world!"
~ Mahatma Gandhi

It is our turn.

January 20, 2020 - NAACP Health Information Dissemination

I am a life time member of the NAACP. My goal is to end poverty and I believe that the more information the community has about the food and drinks they consume, the healthier choices they can make which will also reduce our health cost. To inform the community, I propose that we disseminate the recommended healthy daily amounts of calories, fat, cholesterol, sodium, and sugar. The unhealthy consumption of these ingredients are some of the main reasons why we have heart attacks, strokes, and diabetes.

To disseminate the health information we can create our own media platform by using Facebook, YouTube, Twitter, Instagram, Crisis magazine which is going digital, black newspapers, TV stations, radio, High School and college newsletters.
Also if the Oakland NAACP does not have a newsletter we could start one and advertise there.

We can inundate the community with health information.

Chapter 4 NAACP

Health Information:
TV ads should give health information on the amount of calories, fat, cholesterol, sodium, and sugar in each serving. Special warnings in audio and visual should be provided to those with diabetes, high blood pressure, and high cholesterol levels.

Healthier employees can help create jobs.
Companies who pay healthcare will save money because their employees will be healthier and use less health costs. Companies will have more money to invest in new products and services which would add employment.

Elie Parker

Note:
Other contacts:
State and federal officials.

Superintendent of schools California and other states.

January 22, 2020 - National Reading Label Day

To inform the public of the health risk, we should issue a health alert. To accomplish this, we should be able to use the Oakland NAACP email list.

Also using the Crisis magazine and the national NAACP email list would greatly facilitate the distribution of the health alert.

January 27, 2020 - Health Alert

National Reading Label Day Campaign.

Heart attacks, strokes, diabetes, and obesity is at crisis levels. The CDC (Center for Disease Control) reports that
47% of blacks are obese, 46% of Hispanic, 38% of whites and 12% of Asians. Diabetes plagues 20% of blacks, 21% of Hispanic, 13% of whites, and 14% of Asians. Hypertension or high blood pressure shows blacks at 42%, Hispanic 29%, white 28%, and Asian 27%.

Chapter 4 NAACP

These outcomes can be improved if we read the nutrition labels on the food and drink we consume and follow the daily recommended amounts of the following: calories, fat, cholesterol, sodium, and sugar.

Healthy people live longer, have fewer illnesses, and pay $1,400 less for health costs.
Knowing what's in the food you eat is an easy and cheap way to improve your life.
Consult with your physician to determine your healthy level of consumption.

The amount of ingredients you consume could vary based on your race. For instance, because Blacks are more susceptible to high blood pressure, they should consume sodium on the lower level of the recommended daily nutrition.

Information never killed anyone but certainly the lack of information can. The more we know about what's in the food we eat, the healthier we will be.

Read your way to a healthier and richer person.

Chapter 5 - Media

April 28, 2013 - Sport Analyst & Talk Show Host Influence on Young People

Young African-American boys have some of the lowest reading scores in the nation and some of the highest incarceration and murder rates in the nation. One reason for this condition is the fact that they are constantly exposed to negative images and poor speech. Their neighborhoods are replete with gang activity, drug dealer's attire, broken families, imprisoned fathers, and little encouragement to get an education and progress. Many are not even aware that there is a completely different type of world outside of their trash filled street and poor speaking communities.

That is why it is so important that Black people on television present a positive image and use standard English, not Ebonics or poor speech. The only chance many young people have to experience a progressive environment is when they are taken out of their environment by watching television. Often the programs young Black boys are watching are sports.

Black girls also need positive images as do all girls who live in poor communities.

Listed below are some of the shows that present Black people in a negative way:
NBC Basketball, ESPN Basketball, TNT, ABC - The View, FOX - Glee, NCIS, and The Steve Harvey Show.

To ensure that television presents a positive image of Black and poor people the following should happen:

Black sport analyst and talk show host should speak standard English. They should not have shaved heads, broken or gapped teeth, and their attire should be current and modern. No super fly suits. Men should have business or professional hair cuts. Also men should not wear earring.

Black women should speak standard English, have business or professional hair styles and not be overweight.

Poor English equals poor grades. Exposure is important. The more positive the exposure, the more positive the results in school, business, and life.

July 29, 2013 - Don Lemon

I agree with your opinion that African Americans need to be more responsible.

I have written a book titled "No Excuses - A Guide Out of Poverty" found on Amazon. com. It is my belief that the African American or anyone who is most in need, need to do the most to get out of poverty.

If you send me your address, I will send you a free copy. I hope that you will share the book with your listeners.

February 5, 2014 - Shaved Heads

What does AT&T, and others have in common? Based on their ads, they must think that all Black men have shaved heads. They probably also think that we are all basketball players. Two of the most prominent Black men in the country, President of the United States Obama, and the Attorney General of the United States Holder are not shaved headed, but these companies do not seem to want to present a Black man with their image.

Racism could be at the core of the problem. Or it could be that these companies do not know the Black community.

March 2, 2014 - So Proud to Be a Slave

The movie industry is one of the most racist institution in America. It has a history of casting Black people in submissive roles. They started early with their efforts to cast Black people as an inferior race. One of their opening shows, Amos and Andy presented Blacks as clowns and buffoons.

Chapter 5 Media

Also in the early movies or on television, Black roles were often as servants, as in the Jack Benny show. When a car is involved in a movie, Blacks were not the passenger but the chauffeur, as in the movie Driving Miss Daisy. When trains played a part of the movie, Blacks were the porters carrying someone else's bag. Currently, the slave movies are the toast of the town in Hollywood. From Roots to Amistad to Django Unchained to Twelve Years a Slave, the submissive roles continue.

So what does Hollywood think of Black people, well based on their movies they produce, Blacks are clowns, buffoons, servants, and slaves. Hollywood has now unleashed its most racist weapon, the Academy Awards. Awarding the movie Twelve Years a Slave as the picture of the year is a compilation of a century of showing Black people in submissive roles. To make matters worse, many Blacks will celebrate this travesty. They must be so proud to be a slave.

April 2, 2014 - Thank you for considering my letter to the editor "Affordable Care Act".

I regret that the USA Today exclusivity policy may prevent you from publishing my letter. I hope the newspaper will change its policy to allow other media outlets to publish not just my letter, but any other letter to the editor. Limiting communications to only one media outlet prevents a wider dissemination of ideals and information, a process that is essential to preserving and ensuring a lasting Democracy.

July 31, 2014 - Wolff and Credibility

Dear: Richard D. Wolff

I listened to your broadcast on KPFA on July 25, 2014 comparing President Roosevelt to President Obama. You suggested that FDR was great and Obama was not, because FDR was elected four times. You failed to mention that after FDR's four victories, the 22nd Amendment to the Constitution was passed to prevent anyone from running for President for more than two times.

Chapter 5 Media

I listen to you because I find that most other news outlets do not tell the whole truth. I hope that you do not become one of them.

News comes and goes, but truth and credibility is what defines a person.

September 11, 2014 - White on Rice

I have watched the video of Janay Palmer now married to Ray Rice, the running back for the Baltimore Ravens football team, fighting in the elevator. No man should hit a woman and Ray has apologize. He has also been fired from the team. Janay has come out in defense of her husband and has also said that the media has played up the story to get ratings. I agree with her on the ratings game, but I believe that there is something more sinister at play. I believe that racism may also be fueling the voluminous coverage of this domestic quarrel.

Recently when CHP cop Daniel Andrew who is White repeatedly punched Marlene Pinnock, a Black woman, on the Los Angeles freeway, there was no national outcry or hardly any national press coverage. When the quarterback of the Pittsburgh Steelers football team, Ben Roethlisberger, who is White, was accused of rape, he was not prosecuted. When Kobe Bryant of the LA Lakers and Mike Tyson the boxer were accused of rape, they were both prosecuted. Kobe was found not guilty, but Mike Tyson was sent to jail. When Brett Favre, who previously quarterbacked the Greenbay Packers was caught sending nude photos of himself over the internet, he was not admonished, but given a jean advertising contract. When Bill Belichick, the coach of the New England Patriots football team was caught stealing signals from his opponent, he was not fired, but applauded as being one of the greatest coaches of our time. When Jerry Jones, the owner of the Dallas Cowboys was accused of sexual assault, there was no mention of it during the recent San Francisco-Dallas game, but the game announcers had plenty to say about Ray Rice.There seems to be a double standard. White players and owners who are accused are seldom prosecuted, but Black players are gone after with an vengeance. It seems that those who have failed to defeat the Black players on the field are now trying to vilify them in the courts and the media.

Chapter 5 Media

Poor Black men seem to be getting the worst of it. Some cops have appointed themselves as the judge, jury, and executioner. Their street injustice has resulted in the shooting death of Trayvon Martin in Sanford, FL, Oscar Grant in Oakland, CA and Michael Brown in Ferguson, MO., and many others. If Ray Rice is not allowed to earn a living playing football, he too could join the ranks of the poor Black men unable to defend themselves against an injustice system and just simply shot down in the street. The justice system needs to be audited and changed to ensure justice for all.

Black people must unite. They can not depend on fair coverage in the White controlled media as long as racism is around. Blacks must build their own media outlets to present an accurate image of Black people.

I hope that Janay and Ray lower the gloves and work things out. John Lennon once said that only love counts. Also I hope to see Ray back on the field soon.

October 12, 2014 - NFL TV Coverage

I was watching the Miami - Green Bay football game on the tv station FOX on October 12, 2014. The White quarterback Rodgers throw a touchdown pass to the Black receiver Cobb. The camera crew first put the cameras on Rodgers and the commentator praised Rodgers. Then the cameras when to the White receiver Nelson who had nothing to do with the touchdown, but still he appeared to get credit for the score. Finally the camera was briefly put on Cobb who actually caught the pass.

To further discredit the Black receiver's accomplishment, the commentators declared that the only reason that Cobb had caught seven touchdowns is because of Rodgers. Even when Blacks do well, their achievements are discredited at least on the Fox network. Sam Rosen & John Lynch

The National Football League and the FCC need to investigate and eliminate any racism it finds in broadcasting. The Fox network also needs to ensure that it does not promote racism.

Chapter 5 Media

October 7, 2016 - Black man's hair

What has happened to the black man's hair (see Capital One's ad below). The Afro, once the symbol of racial pride and defiance has been shaved off. Most African-American men in the movies, TV shows, advertisements, commercials, and online has had to shave off their hair which can be a dehumanizing, humiliating, and a psychological method of controlling them.

Also black actors are required to adorn themselves with women earrings and speak poor English, even though many can speak English very well. It's no wonder that many of the black youth listening and watching the television or going to the movies can't get through the 12th grade.

Watch and listen and whenever one of these shaved headed blacks appear, remember your well-being is not what they have in mind.

Also from what century did Capital One get those glasses for Samuel Jackson to wear in their ad? A company without a future is forever living in the past.

Chapter 5 Media

July 3, 2018 - Claws, the TV show on TNT is racist.

The show features Black people acting, looking, and talking like they have never gone to school, or they are unaware of the twenty first century. Speaking lines from the Black actresses include:

Where we going?
What you mean?
I ain't gonna die in this outfit.
Y'all too.
What you doing here?

Children and adults hearing and repeating this type of poor English will have little chance in the academic world or any other progressive endeavors, such as building companies, universities, or financial investments.

Portraying Blacks as unable to speak English and as out-of-date misfits only adds to the racial stereotypes that Hollywood is known for. We need to reject this Black exploitation show and all the other shows, movies, and companies that denigrate Blacks or any one else. Only when all people are treated with respect can the nation and the world move forward.

January 28, 2019 - Shaved heads again

What does Geico, AT&T, Capital One, Microsoft, Audi, Whole Foods, Toyota Entertainment, Tonight (ET), Sprint, Persil ProClean, Floor and Decor, Saatva, Wayfair, and Zantac have in common? They all have at least one shaved head Black man. The white men in the ads or show have their hair. They look more like doctors, engineers, and professors. Not many in this group have shaved heads. The black man with their shaved heads look more like basketball or football players.

The companies showing black men with shaved heads seem to think that black people can only relate to ball players. This gives a subliminal message to young black people that their careers are limited to sports and not the academics.

Chapter 5 Media

Less than 1% of all careers are in professional sports. The other 99% are in careers outside of sports. Young people need to embrace the academics. That is where the future is.

Hollywood, the media and corporate America loves to show shaved headed Black men. The media is full of them. It appears that in order for a Black man to get on television he has to shave off his hair. It appears to be the same dehumanizing tactic the Nazis used to dehumanize the Jews. It made killing them seem less barbaric.

The White police officer in Chicago who shot the Black youth 16 times probably did not see a human being. He was probably indoctrinated by the media to see the black youth as less than a human.

America has done almost everything it could to make Black people seem to be inhuman. African-Americans have been vilified, ostracize and segregated. Millions of them have been relegated to the slums and prisons of America.

The media has been the main instrument to deliver this relentless message of bigotry and racism. African-Americans need to counter this negative image of Blacks with their own positive image. In order to accomplish this, African Americans must own their own news, movie, and TV media. We can build a media that reflects the humans that we really are.

February 24, 2019 - Black face and Harvard university

Your article on the black face and Hollywood was very insightful. Hollywood has long been a place for stereotypes and racism. From the Amos and Andy show to the current movies and TV shows little has changed. Blacks shown as maids and butlers has permeated the Hollywood mantra. Racism is a little bit more subtle in today's movies and TV shows. Also black actors are required to give testimony to the tremendous accomplishments of the white actors on the screen.

Chapter 5 Media

Often the white actors are saving the world or doing extraordinary things such as leaping tall buildings in a single bound as in superman for instance. Blacks on the other hand are shown as uncertain and confused and in need of guidance and help from their white counterparts.

Showing blacks as weak and whites as superior in strength, knowledge and ambition is a stereotype that has inundated practically every institution and every mind in America. If America is to survive it must end racism. Racism and democracy is not compatible.

Chapter 6 - Education

April 8, 2020 - Broken English

Speaking or writing broken English seems like a prescription for failure. After all, 99% of the nation's textbooks are written in standard English. If you don't know standard English, there's little chance you will be able to read science, math or even English books. Without book knowledge, you'll be relegated to the portals of poverty. So study, learn, and use standard English. It is the pathway to success.

April 21, 2020 - Prisons Before Schools

The United States, a nation that will build prisons before they will build schools.

Prisons prisons everywhere. Education nowhere near. Politicians who do not care. Prisons prisons everywhere.

May 29, 2020 - Sports and Education for Blacks

As millions of blacks and others go into sports, only a small percentage go on to professional careers, what about the rest. How many Blacks and other players graduate? What type of degrees do they earn? Does sports in college come before academics? Coaches are paid large salaries why not players? If a player does not receive a quality education does that mean they are unpaid? In the past we call that slavery.

College sports need reform. Players should be compensated for their work on the field and receive a quality education.

Chapter 6 Education

May 29, 2020 - Northeastern Ohio. Buckeyes everywhere.

My time at South High was not a very productive one. Although I signed up for advanced classes in science, math, and English, my overseer's all White decided that I would be more at home in the steel mills that permeated the Mahoning Valley.

Instead of college prep classes, I was given factory prep classes. They included machine shop, metal shop, and wood shop. I had no aptitude or interest for any of these shops. My education was rounded out with music and gym classes, also no attitude. I think they put me in these classes because I was black, a practice I believe is still going on today since there seem to be so few blacks in math or science careers.

Because of my lack of college prep courses as mentioned above, and lack of money, I did not think I had any chance of going to college. I did ask my school counselor should I go to college and the answer was no, after all, I had been educated for the steel mills. Also I took a bookkeeping class and I asked the teacher are there any jobs in bookkeeping. Again the answer was no, although there were millions of jobs in bookkeeping.

All of my teachers in high school were white and I think what the white instructors was telling me was that there were no jobs for blacks in white-collar office jobs. Given this discouragement to go to college, I decided to enter the Marine Corps.

The Marine Corps office was on the north side of my town and in between that office and my home was a university. I remember the day well. As I headed to the marine office, I had to stop at an intersection because of a red light. The intersection just happen to be at the administrative office of Youngstown University, now Youngstown State University.

I thought to myself could this be a sign that I should go to college. Further I thought what do I have to lose so I entered the administrative building. I went to the admissions window and asked can I apply?

Chapter 6 Education

Now let's remember I've been told by my school counselor, teachers, friends, and family that I could not get into college. I had fully expected the admissions person to call the dogs and have me chased down through the halls of the institution. I was shocked when the administer asked me what did I want to take. He didn't ask me if I was qualified, he didn't ask me if I had taken college prep courses, he didn't ask me if I had taken the college entrance exam.

It was probably the first time in my life that a roadblock had not been thrown in front of me. After seven years of day and night school, I graduated from Youngstown State University with a BSBA in Accounting and Economics and my life was changed forever. Education took me from poverty to wealth and I am forever grateful to YSU. Education is the key to success and everyone should be given that opportunity.

Chapter 7 - Gun Control

December 14, 2012 - Repeal the 2nd Amendment

The 2nd Amendment supposedly gives a citizen the right to bear arms. In 2010, that right allowed us to murder 8,775 of our fellow citizens, including men, women, and children with firearms. Our latest murders at the Sandy Hook Elementary school took the lives of 20 children. Haven't we had enough of the 2nd Amendment and firearms? We are suppose to be an advanced country but are acting like we are still living on the frontier. We don't need guns any longer to hunt for our meat. The grocery stores have plenty. The Indians are no longer burning our homes and farms. The biggest threat the Indians pose today is a rigged roulette table.

In Britain, citizens are not allowed to own firearms and their murder rate is a fraction of ours. Although they are 1/5 the size of the US, in 2010 they had 58 murders by firearms. In 2012, Oakland, CA, alone have twice that many. If we feel that we need protection from home invaders, street thugs, or wild animals, we have and can develop less lethal weapons like taser or stun guns, or chemical discharge devices or even concussion grenades. It is time for the nation to move into the 21 century and repeal the 2nd Amendment and save lives.

January 13, 2013 - Gun Control

Even when 20 first graders are gunned down, there is no national outcry for gun control. Sure there were cards and teddy bears sent to the Sandy Hook elementary school. Even some sport teams around the country had a moment of silence, but the big reaction from the shooting was a spike in gun sales.

Violence is now our new entertainment. It is everywhere, in our movies, tv programs, and video games. Shooting is seen as a sport, a national pastime. There have been so many killings with guns it is hard to tell the difference between what is real and what is entertainment.

Chapter 7 Gun Control

January 16, 2013 - Gun Free Society

Let't get real. The only way to protect ourselves from gun violence is to get rid of the guns. The suggested ways of stopping gun violence include background checks, increased mental help, reduced magazine size, and swat teams in every school. Because there are over 300 million guns in the United States, these suggestions will not stop a mass killer. If a mentally deranged person wants to get a gun, there are plenty around.

Most murders are not mass killings, but one on one, and there are some other steps we can take to reduce that number. Fifty percent of the people involved in violent crimes do not have a high school degree. Another forty percent have no college hours. Based on these numbers, if high school students go on to college the murder rate will drop by ninety percent.

Ending poverty and improving the schools will ensure that every student is ready for college. Another step we can take is to require an annual gun registration fee. This will reduce the number of guns on the street. To stop the mass killings, America will have to move to a gun free society.

The profile of a mass killer is so diverse It is almost impossible to know who the future killers are and to prevent another mass murder like the one what occurred at the Sandy Hook Elementary school that killed twenty children and six adults. We need to repeal the 2nd Amendment or get a ruling that only the militia has the right to bear arms. Which I think it said. We can become a gun free society if we focus more on the future rather than on the past.

June 9, 2013 - Santa Monica Killings and the Gun Free Society

The recent killing of five people by a gunman in Santa Monica California demonstrates once again the need for gun control. When a gunman can go up and down the streets shooting and killing people at random, the country can no longer pretend that we are a safe and civilized society.

Chapter 7 Gun Control

Of course, drive by shooting and random shooting are nothing new in America's ghettos, but now they have moved to beachfront communities like Santa Monica and suburban schools like Sandy Hook in Conn., where twenty children were gun downed along with six adults.

We can be consider an advanced and civilized country by breaking with our history of gun ownership. Guns and advancement are mutually exclusive. Moving forward means leaving guns behind. To facilitate this transformation, we will have to eliminate the reason why people think they need a gun to protect themselves.

Since nearly ninety percent of violent crimes are committed by people with limited education the key is to ensure that every person receives a quality education. When this is achieved, we will eliminate most of our crime and the need to own a gun. Also, a gun free society would take the guns out of the hands of the mentally ill which has been a major contributor to the mass killings that have occurred across the country.

May 25, 2018 - Gun Free Society

We are now on the 22nd mass shooting. Prayers and condolences has been offered to the families of the dead and wounded but nothing has been done to stop the killing. The lack of action to stop the shooting suggest that the country has accepted the killing of its children as the price of gun ownership. This is a price too high to pay for any nation that expects to have a future. We need to realize that we have too many guns in the country and that "guns do kill".

The solution is to repeal the Second Amendment and eliminate gun ownership by private citizens. If the United States wants to be a world leader in something other than school shootings, we need to advance into a gun free society.

Chapter 7 Gun Control

December 8, 2017 - To elected leaders: One Killing too Many - Stop the Killing

The response from the authorities to the recent killing of 6 students at the Rancho Tehama Elementary school in California is alarming. Six students dead and the response from the authorities and others is that it could have been worse.

We have gotten so use to mass murders that when only six people are killed we are relieved and almost declare a victory.

In year 2015, 13,286 people were killed and 26,819 injured in the United States by firearms and little has been done to stop the killing. It appears that as a nation, we have become inapt and unwilling to end the killing even when our children's lives are on the line. Mass killing of children has become acceptable.

Our shooting and killing problems are only going to get worse until we act to solve them.

We are not getting much leadership on mass murders from the Federal government, therefore it is up to the States to solve the problem. I recommend that a California commission be instituted to find out why we have shootings and present recommendations on how to stop the killing.

One suggestion that I have is that because 90 percent of most shootings are done by people with a high school diploma or less, we should ensure that everyone receives a quality education greater than a high school degree. Also because some people have guns because they fear others, by educating everyone, that fear would dissipate and we would have fewer guns on the street. In addition, our mental health facilities need to be enhanced to better identify those with mental problems.

When society begins to accept the worse, it becomes the worse. California can be the most progressive state in the union, we only have to think and act that way.

Chapter 7 Gun Control

February 26, 2018 - Saving the lives of our children who are our future is good business.

Has the United States become such a morally bankrupted country that even the killing of its children does not prompt it to act to stop the slaughter?

Companies that standup and denounce the violence and end their business with the gun industry and their spokespersons, the NRA should be applauded. Companies that supported the gun industry and the NRA should be identified and exposed for the corrupt institutions they have become.

Companies that will sacrifice our children and our nation's future for money to buy their boats and big homes represents the worse we could be.

Chapter 8 - Coronavirus

May 5, 2020 - Coronavirus - The Party is Over

A couple of years back, I was on a cruise liner attending a party. The party was held in the atrium of the ship. The atrium was six stories high, festoon with confetti, balloons, and ribbons. Each level was crowded with people singing, dancing, and drinking. Many of the participants were in tuxedos or long gowns. As I look up at the proceedings, I couldn't help but wonder where did these folks get the money needed to participate in such a ruckus event.

In March 2020, I think I got the answer. Prior to 2020, the nation partied hard and saved little, but in March 2020 because of the coronavirus, businesses in the US shut down. In only one week into the shut down, companies that were paying executives millions and buying back company stock suddenly needed a government handout.

For the businesses, it appears that they did not buy business interruption insurance, so they were not prepared for the pandemic. Also, Individuals who were gainfully employed in February were suddenly unemployed and in bread lines in March. For the individual, the rule that you should have at least six months of reserves apparently was not honored. If there is anything, we have learned from the coronavirus pandemic is that you can hope for the best, but you need to plan for the worst.

For now the Coronavirus has ended the party, only the pain of being unprepared remains.

May 19, 2020 - Coronavirus vs the Beach

What's more important than going to the beach in 2020? What's more important is going to the beach in 2021. The beach will be there in 2021, will you be?

Chapter 9 - Hate

February 3, 2012 - Gay Marriage

We can find so many ways to hate each other, i.e., the color of a person's skin, a person's religion, a person's birthplace, and a person's choice of who they marry. A Feb 2, 2012 Letter to the Editor of the San Leandro Times concerning same sex marriage suggested that this type of union will lead to the degeneration of nature and threaten humanity. Since the beginning of time, the threat to humanity has not come from same sex marriages but from hate and fear.

Hate and fear fermented by exaggerated claims of imminent society destruction. Hate against Blacks, Jews, Hispanics, Asians, Gays, and anyone who might seem different or come from some other place or don't follow the established way is the real threat to society. Humanity would be better served if we reject hate and fear and embrace each person for who they our. Humanity is actually made weaker when we reject our uniqueness and made stronger when we accept them.

Marriage is a very personal relationship. Each person has the right to love and marry the person of their choice and we should not let hate or fear stand in their way.

July 8, 2018 - Name Calling

Name calling is not the characteristic of strong people. It is the purview of frightened people. Bigotry can come in many colors. We should not become so bitter that the very thing we want to replace we become.

Chapter 10 - Leadership

January 24, 2013 - President Barack Obama

Great Presidents do great things. There is nothing greater than ensuring that there is justice and equality for all. We support you in this endeavor.

September 6, 2013 - Syria - With Leadership comes responsibility

The United States is known as a world leader. This recognition did not come by avoiding difficult problems but by addressing them. Also it did not come by always making the right or easy decision. Currently, most would agree that going into Iraq or Afghanistan was not the best decision. On the other hand, many would agree that fighting Nazi Germany was the right decision. We should judge each situation on its own set of facts and determine what is the best course of action to advance the human race.

December 12, 2019 - Trump has violated the Golden Rule

The Golden Rule as stated in the Old Testament: Leviticus 19:18 ("Thou shalt not avenge, nor bear any grudge against the children of thy people, but thou shalt love thy neighbor as thyself).

Elie's addendum to the Golden Rule:

Thou shalt not discriminate against Blacks in housing as Trump has done. Thou shalt not issue worthless degrees at Trump University. Thou shalt not steal from charities as the Trump's foundation did. Thou shalt not endorse white supremacist. Thou shalt not assert that he Trump can grab or molest any woman. Thou shalt not ban people because they are Muslim. Thou shalt not declare that Mexicans are rapists and murderers. Thou shalt not cage children and separate them from their parents. Thou shalt not denigrate the American justice system by claiming that he, Trump could shoot someone on fifth Avenue and not be held responsible or accountable.

Chapter 10 Leadership

Thou shalt not jeopardized our national security by accepting the Russians' spy agency assessment over our own security agencies. Thou shalt not start a trade war on every continent, balloon the deficit, ignore climate change or weakened NATO.

Trump has not only violated the golden rule, but has attempted to spread fear, racism and hatred on a level unseen since the Nazis occupied Germany. Our prayers should not be to endorse Trump's behavior, but to bury it and send Trump into immediate retirement or impeachment and removal from office, which ever comes first.

Chapter 11 - International

July 28, 2014 - Fairness in Israel and Palestine Coverage

I was watching the news coverage of the Israel and Palestine conflict and appears that the Israelis are getting favorable coverage. Even through the Israelis are the occupation force in Gaza and the Palestinians live under the iron boot of the Israelis, the coverage suggest that the Jewish state is only trying to protect itself from the unwarranted claims of the people they drove out of their homes.

The tunnels are a case in point. The news coverage infers that the tunnels dug by the Palestinians are only used to move fighters into Gaza. The coverage fail to mention that the tunnels are also used to bring in food and other supplies to the Palestinians who are under an Israeli blockage.

The land grab by Israel after the 1967 war is not recognized by the United Nation, but in order to support that illegal action some are compelled to justify another illegal act such as the killing of over 1,000 Palestinian men, women, and children.

At some point, the integrity or the lack of it on the part of the news coverage comes into question. Supporting what is wrong will not make it right, but will make it worse.

July 30, 2014 - Don Lemon

Peace is at hand, the Israelis only have to share it with the Palestinians.

By the way, your comment that you do not bring rocks to a gun fight, let us not forget that David only had rocks against Goliath.

Chapter 11 International

July 30, 2014 - Liz Kearney

In Vietnam, why would the Vietcong attack our tanks with sticks? Probably the same reason the Palestinians go to the roof tops during an air attack. Desperate times call for desperate measures.

August 15, 2014 - Israelis and Palestinians - The Two State Solution

Previously I wrote a letter stating that the Israelis and Palestinians must share the land. The response I received ranges from the unprintable to California Senator Dianne Feinstein who supports a two state solution. Dianne realizes that sharing the land can lead to fairness and equality which will triumph over fear and conflict.

The immediate goal now is to achieve the two state solution. The United Nation who created Israel and the United States who is Israel's main supporter need to force a settlement on the two parties. My recommendations would be to establish a viable Palestinian state. Israel would return to the borders recognized by the United Nations.

To maximize border security, land swaps between the parties would be allowed if both agree. The right of the Palestinians to return home would be part of the agreement. The percentage of returning Palestinians would be set so that it does not endanger the status of the Jewish state. Payments would be made to the Palestinians who chose not to return or who can not return. The payments to the Palestinians would be commensurate to their property and psychological lost. The right to exist for both the Israeli and Palestinian states would be guaranteed by the United Nation.

Wars every few years between Israelis and Palestinians only builds more hate on both sides. Let's end the hate and embrace the two state solution.

Chapter 11 International

July 21, 2014 - The Children are Coming. The Children are Coming. Run for your lives.

The United States is a nation of immigrants. Without past immigration, the United States would not exist. Without future immigration, the USA population will decline as it has in Japan and many other nations who has strict immigration policies.

We should not fear the children from Honduras or any other immigrant for they bring new blood, new skills, and new aspirations. There are millions of immigrant who are overachievers in the United States. One of our latest immigrants Musk is building electric cars in United States and rockets to resupply the international space station.

Let us open up our borders to all who would come. It would benefit them as well as us.

The Europeans working through the EU have already opened up their borders with its member nations, the United States should adopt a similar approach with our neighbors.

Open borders means open hearts for them and for us.

September 21, 2019 - Brexit

For centuries the armies of Europe have marched across each other's borders in countless wars and conflicts. Finally in 1957, the European nations decided to stop fighting each other and start trading with each other. They formed what is now called the European Union or the EU. For over 60 years, that union has prevented major wars in Europe and has brought prosperity to the Continent.

Brexit, which is England's attempt to leave the EU threatens that prosperity and peace. Britain, the nation that once boasted that the sun never sets on the Union Jack and at one time built an empire that stretched from Hong Kong to the Carolinas, now appears to be gripped in fear of world involvement.

Chapter 11 International

The Brexit supporters' attempt to pull up the drawbridges and create a moat around England will only isolate it militarily and economically. England should not surrender to fear of change, fear of growth or fear of world leadership. England should remain in the European Union. It has been and will continue to be the path to peace and prosperity in England, Europe and the rest of the world.

When and where did it start that people felt they should fear each other? One possible starting point is the contrived belief that one person is better than another person. The belief that I am better than you can metastasize into many forms such as my religion is better than your religion or my race is better than your race or that my place of origin is better than your place of origin. Differentiating can easily translate in to fear and prejudices.

The European Union had it right and represents the blueprint for world peace. They took down their borders and realized that respecting the person is more important and more productive than fighting over land.

October 8, 2019 - NBA in China

In the defense of profits over the defense of human rights, America should always be on the side of human rights.

Dear Mr. Morey
Your apology for standing up for human rights is not accepted. Rockets general manager Daryl Morey tweeted support for the anti-government protestors in Hong Kong.

NBA Houston Rockets versus the Chinese communist.
In the defense of human right apologies are not necessary.

October 15, 2019 - Hong Kong Protest

Good to hear from you Christian. I hope all is going well. I think that we all agree that human rights is the ultimate goal for everyone, it's just a matter of how we achieve it.

Chapter 11 International

In a democracy, individuals, governments and corporations are equally responsible for ensuring human rights not only in America but throughout the world. After all, we hold ourselves out as the leader of the free world and as they say, freedom is not free. Sometimes you have to pay for it in the form of giving up profits to ensure human rights.

US Manufacturing:

As to manufacturing in the United States, I think that train has left the station. Unskilled and semi skilled jobs are best done in developing countries. They can do it cheaper and corporations will always and must always look for the cheapest labor cost to stay competitive not only in the United States but throughout the world. Because we are a nation of immigrants, we can draw from the world some of the best brain power. That makes us a world leader in innovation, science, finance, and most important human rights. That's something the Chinese communist can never achieve.

January 30, 2020 - UK exits the EU - a hollow victory

The UK leaving the EU is a defeat even though it's dressed up like a victory. The UK, now replete with isolationist and segregationist is trying to seal its self off from the rest of the world in hopes of returning to the past, when England was whiter, its religions purer, and its peasants knew their place. The glow of Prime Minister Johnson resurrection will soon come face to face with evolution. A force not controlled by men, but the insatiable force of nature that distributes the earth's people and assets in a manner conducive to its survival.

May 27, 2020 - World without Borders

In the year 1943, I entered this troubled planet, and the world was at war. By that year, the allies were taking the war to the axis. The Japanese have been turned back at Midway, the Germans had failed to cross the English channel and the Russians were staunchly defending the outskirts of Leningrad.

Chapter 11 International

There were two more years of heavy fighting but the writing was on the wall. The Americans, Russians, British, French and their allies would overwhelm the Germans, Italians and Japanese and set a new world order. I was born in the middle of that war and I have known nothing else but nations fighting nations, religions fighting religions, and people fighting people.

Although millions of lives were lost during the second world war, some good things have come out of the chaos. One, the United Nations was born which gave countries a chance to take their grievances before a world body and possibly seek solutions before turning to the instruments of war. Another major advancement was the creation of the European Union or the EU. Before the EU, the European countries had been fighting each other for centuries.

Since the creation of the EU, most of western Europe has been at peace. They have traded in their instruments of war for commerce and trade and they have all prospered. In the process, they have become a borderless society with commerce and trade freely moving between their members. It is a model that other countries should adopt. In fact at some point I would hope that borders would disappear throughout the world. After all, borders are a creation of man, designed to pit tribes against tribes, religions against religions, and people against people all to feather the nest of a few potentates. The world without borders is a world at peace.

Chapter 12 - Conflict of Interest

The appearance of what is true doesn't always represent reality. Often there can be a conflict of interest which does not appear on the surface but lingers below the surface out of sight and out of mind. Listed below are some organizations and activities that should be reviewed to ensure that they do not have a conflict of interest.

1. Police and crime reduction: How much does it cost to incarcerate? Do the police, courts, judges, prisons benefit when the crime rate goes up? Do they have a disincentive to reduce crime?

2. Education and graduation: Should teachers and superintendent salary be based on the graduation rate and SAT scores.

3. Charities and poverty reduction: How much of the donations go to the poor and how much to the administrators?

4. Church and peace: Do religions vilify other religions to build up membership? After centuries, why can't different religions learn to live with each other?

5. Campaign contributions and voting record: Pay for play. Government projects and contracts should be identified with any campaign contributors.

6. Sales and profits: Should sports programs accept dangerous and unhealthy products like booze?

7. Doctors and patients: The healthier the patient the less medical attention is required. Do doctors and hospitals have an incentive to keep patients unhealthy? Also are doctors paid by the types and number of pills they recommend?

Chapter 12 Conflict of Interest

8   Lottery money for schools: How much of the lottery money actually goes to the schools? Is it a plus or minus from the general funds? Does lottery promotion promote gambling and what is the social cost?

9   War profiteering: Who profits from wars? Government officials and corporations should be identified if they profit from wars.

10   Sports in college: Some student athletes don't even go to class. Are they discourage from taking harder majors? How many graduate and with what degrees?

11   Marijuana versus profits: Does the taxes collected from marijuana sales pay for the cost of using marijuana. The cost would include loss of work time, loss of employment, loss of health, and loss of income.

Conclusion

June 20, 2020 - The End of the USA Empire?

In a stew of stupidity and fear, the end could be approaching for the United States. Where there's strength in unity, there is weakness in separation and the USA is one of the most segregated nations on the planet. Whites live with Whites, Blacks with Blacks, Hispanics with Hispanics, and Asians with Asians.

At this point, racism can be found in almost every institution in the country including segregated churches, bias police forces, museums and art galleries, political parties, corporate board rooms, school boards, college entrance exams, banks, insurance companies, advertising agencies, the media, and governments.

Racism is structurally embedded in these organizations and only a radical approach would unhinge years of bigotry. The nation has tried affirmative action and diversity, but both have failed to end racism. If the nation was serious about ending racism it could institute a quota system. An approach that would require measurable results.

African Americans who have been excluded from the nation's economy must build their own economic system. It must be large enough to compete with the White, Asian and Hispanic economies. At some point you would hope that these economies can all merge otherwise the nation will drift apart along racial lines, a process that has already started. It could mark the end of the USA Empire.

The End of an Empire:
Some empires die from outside conquerors and some die from the rot within. The rot that could break up the USA is racism which could carve up the country along geographic and racial lines. Progressive and liberal White America will take the midwest and Northeast. Black Americans and Latinos will take the south east. Hispanics and Native Americans will take the southwest including Los Angeles. Asians, white liberals, and Pacific Islanders will take Northern California and the rest of the West Coast, and White segregationist will move to the mountain states.

Conclusion

The question is, will the United States still be united or will it copy Yugoslavia which broke up into six different countries, mainly over economic and ethnic differences?

There could be hope. In 1965, my college professor told me and the class that the way to solve the race problem in the United States was interracial marriages. New marriages in the USA between races are 15%. This compares with 8% of current marriages.

The trend looks good.

The United States is at a crossroad. It can choose to be a racist and segregated nation or a democracy. The two choices are mutually exclusive.

Choose well.

Bibliography

Acknowledgments

Special thanks to my wife Aris who did the first edit of the book.

Bibliography

Chapter 2 Wealth

1. Juliana Horowitz - Pew Research
2. Poverty rate per "Talk poverty.org"

Chapter 3 Health

1. Niaz Kasravi
2. Pastor Delman Coates on Coca-Cola dangers
3. Pastor William Lamar on Coca-Cola dangers
4. Erika Edwards - Low fat diet reduces risk of dying from breast cancer.
5. CNN article by Dr. William Schaffer - What soap and warm water do to the coronavirus.

Chapter 5 Media

1. Richard D. Wolff - Wolff and Credibility
2. Hilary O. Shelton Advocate NAACP

Index

12 Down. How many to go? c1 p11

African Americans and People of Color Need an Agenda of their Own c2 p35

African-American Poverty Rate c2 p37

Affordable Care Act (ACA) c3 p46

Bill Cosby was right. c2 p31

Black boy shot by White Cop c1 p11

Black face and Harvard university c5 p77

Black man's hair c5 p75

Blacks in College c6 p79

Black Lives Matter - Do They? c1 p23

Black people will get out of poverty. c2 p39

Brexit c11 p93

Broken English c6 p79

Build Baby Build c2 p26

Charlottesville c1 p15

Children are coming c11 p93

Claws, The TV show on TNT is racist c5 p76

Clyde W. Vaughan Jr. c2 p34

Index

Coca-Cola c3 p48

Colin Kaepernick and racial injustice c2 p30

Confederate Statues come tumbling down. c1 p22

Cornell William Brooks c4 p64

Coronavirus - A Killer c3 p55

Coronavirus - Prevention c3 p54

Coronavirus - The Party is Over c8 p87

Corona versus the Beach c8 p87

Dear Commissioner Silver c1 p11

Donations c1 p35

Don Lemon - Peace is at hand between Israel and the Palestinians c11 p91

Don Lemon - Those with the most wealth receive the most justice. c1 p13

Don Lemon - African-American's Responsibility c5 p71

Economic Opportunity is best served Black c4 p62

Economic Opportunity is best served with Self-Determination c4 p65

Fairness in Israel and Palestinian coverage c11 p91

Ferguson, MO Shooting Never Again c1 p12

Index

Fiscal Cliff & the Veterans of Foreign Wars (VFW) c3 p44

Flip Phones to Wealth c2 p24

Gay marriage c9 p88

Gambling exploitation of the Poor c2 p37

George Floyd Killing - Past time for Blacks to Act c1 p17

George Holland - President Oakland NAACP c4 p66

Grand Conspiracy - Institutionalized Poverty c2 p33

Gun Control c7 p82

Gun Free Society c7 p83

Gun Free Society 22nd Mass Shooting c7 p84

Health Alert c3 p53

Health Alert - Read the Label Campaign c4 p67

Health Causes c3 p53

Health Chart c3 p46

Health information c3 p51

Health Responsibilities c3 p45

Hilary O. Shelton c4 p62

Hong Kong Protest c11 p94

Index

Coca-Cola c3 p48

Colin Kaepernick and racial injustice c2 p30

Confederate Statues come tumbling down. c1 p22

Cornell William Brooks c4 p64

Coronavirus - A Killer c3 p55

Coronavirus - Prevention c3 p54

Coronavirus - The Party is Over c8 p87

Corona versus the Beach c8 p87

Dear Commissioner Silver c1 p11

Donations c1 p35

Don Lemon - Peace is at hand between Israel and the Palestinians c11 p91

Don Lemon - Those with the most wealth receive the most justice. c1 p13

Don Lemon - African-American's Responsibility c5 p71

Economic Opportunity is best served Black c4 p62

Economic Opportunity is best served with Self-Determination c4 p65

Fairness in Israel and Palestinian coverage c11 p91

Ferguson, MO Shooting Never Again c1 p12

Index

Fiscal Cliff & the Veterans of Foreign Wars (VFW) c3 p44

Flip Phones to Wealth c2 p24

Gay marriage c9 p88

Gambling exploitation of the Poor c2 p37

George Floyd Killing - Past time for Blacks to Act c1 p17

George Holland - President Oakland NAACP c4 p66

Grand Conspiracy - Institutionalized Poverty c2 p33

Gun Control c7 p82

Gun Free Society c7 p83

Gun Free Society 22nd Mass Shooting c7 p84

Health Alert c3 p53

Health Alert - Read the Label Campaign c4 p67

Health Causes c3 p53

Health Chart c3 p46

Health information c3 p51

Health Responsibilities c3 p45

Hilary O. Shelton c4 p62

Hong Kong Protest c11 p94

Index

Inequality in America and what to do about it c1 p17

Israel and the Palestinians c11 p91

Israelis and Palestinians - The Two State Solution c11 p92

Justice is not Free c1 p14

Justice is for sale in America and you need the money to buy it. c1 p14

Katrina and early coronavirus warning ignored. c2 p41

Kent State shooting c1 p16

Killing of Ahmad Aubrey and Justice in America c1 p16

Lady in the woods c2 p39

Lawless c1 p16

Liz Kearney - Desperate times call for desperate measures c1 p92

Low fat diet reduce risk of breast cancer c3 p49

Marijuana, supposedly harmless drug c2 p40

Marijuana c3 p51

Mary Radcliffe - donations to newspapers c2 p35

NAACP's Agenda c4 p61

NAACP and NBA Owner Donald Sterling c4 p59

Index

NAACP Focus c4 p59

NAACP Health Alert c4 p68

NAACP Health, Education, and Wealth c4 p60

NAACP Health Information Dissemination c4 p67

NAACP - Oakland Branch c4 p66

Name Calling c9 p88

Nation of Prisons c6 p79

National Reading Label Day c3 p51

NBA in China c11 p94

NFL The New Patriots c1 p14

NFL TV Coverage c5 p74

Net worth Black versus White c2 p37

Niaz Kasravi c3 p45

Northeastern Ohio. Buckeyes everywhere. C6 p80

One Killing too Many c7 p85

On the video Tara Allen sang ' justice is coming soon' c1 p13

Opportunity in Ownership c2 p26

Power of the Purse and the Confederate Flag c1 p13

President Obama c10 p89

Index

Quality Education Fights Crime and Poverty c7 p84

Racism from Sea to Shining Sea c1 p19

Read and Protect Your Health c3 p54

Real Problem c2 p27

Repeal the 2nd Amendment   c7 p82

Reparation   c3 p56

Richard D. Wolff c2 p24

Richard Wolff and Credibility c5 p72

Richard D. Wolff - Roosevelt versus Obama c5 p72

San Francisco Bay View - Economic Racism c2 p36

Santa Monica Killing in the Gun Free Society c7 p83

Shaved Heads c5 p71

Shaved Heads Again c5 p76

Save Me Slogans c1 p21

Slave Master Mentality c2 p25

Saving the lives of our children c7 p86

Smoking & Ebony c3 p47

So Proud to Be a Slave c5 p71

Index

Sport Analyst & Talk Show Host Influence on Young People c5 p70

Sports and Education for Blacks c6 p79

Strengthen the California Menu Labeling Law c3 p47

Syria - With Leadership comes Responsibility c10 p89

Sugar Industry c3 p48

Trayvon's Death Not in Vain c1 p11

Trump has violated the Golden Rule c10 p89

UK exit the EU - a hollow victory c11 p95

USA Today exclusivity policy c5 p72

Vaping c3 p50

Wealth Gap Between Blacks and Whites c2 p27

Wealth will set you free. c2 p38

White on Rice c5 p73

World without Borders c11 p95

You are what you eat. c3 p49

www.ingramcontent.com/pod-product-compliance
Lightning Source LLC
Chambersburg PA
CBHW060423220526
45465CB00008B/2992